# William Faulkner's
# THE SOUND AND THE FURY

## AND OTHER WORKS

### A CRITICAL COMMENTARY

## SAMUEL BECKOFF, Ph.D.

MONARCH
PRESS

Published by
MONARCH PRESS
a Simon & Schuster division of
Gulf & Western Corporation
Simon & Schuster Building
1230 Avenue of the Americas
New York, N.Y. 10020


MONARCH PRESS and colophon are trademarks of
Simon & Schuster, registered in the U.S. Patent and
Trademark Office.

Manufactured in the United States of America

Printed and Bound by Semline, Inc.

ISBN: 0-671-00613-4

# TABLE OF CONTENTS

## NOTE TO THE STUDENT

This Critical Commentary is intended to aid you in your study and appreciation of Faulkner's *The Sound and The Fury*. Other works by Faulkner are treated primarily for the light they throw on the themes and techniques to be found in that major novel. Most of the discussion will make little sense to you unless you are already familiar with the text of at least *The Sound and The Fury*. This Critical Commentary is written with the assumption that it will prompt you continually to *refer back to the original text*. An extensive, annotated bibliography is provided to encourage you to pursue some of the critical questions raised on your own.

*The Editors*

# WILLIAM FAULKNER, PRIVATE CITIZEN, OF OXFORD, LAFAYETTE COUNTY, MISSISSIPPI

William Faulkner, eldest of four sons of Murry Falkner *(sic)* and Maud Butler Falkner, was born on September 25, 1897, at New Albany, Union County, about 35 miles from Oxford, Lafayette County, in the State of Mississippi. Between that date and July 6, 1962, when he died, he spent most of his life in Oxford as a very private citizen, and in Jefferson, Yoknapatawpha County, as a very famous writer. The long period of jealously guarded privacy was made possible when the family moved from New Albany to Oxford in 1902; the long, celebrated period as one of America's greatest novelists was made possible when Faulkner became "sole owner and proprietor" of Yoknapatawpha County through publication in 1929 of *Sartoris*, first of the novels in the Yoknapatawpha series.

FAULKNER'S FATHER. Murry Falkner (like his son later on) dropped out of his class at the University of Mississippi (Ole Miss), moved from one job to another, and at last was given a position as conductor on the family railroad, the job he had when William was born. After the family moved to Oxford, Murry ran a stable for ten years and then worked in the hardware business for eight years. In 1918, after pulling family and friendship strings, he was appointed secretary and business manager at the University of Mississippi (just outside Oxford) and remained in that post until his death.

FAULKNER'S GRANDFATHER. John Wesley Thompson Falkner improved the family railroad and became president of the First National Bank of Oxford.

FAULKNER'S GREAT-GRANDFATHER. Colonel William Cuthbert Falkner (the name was originally spelled Faulkner, but the Colonel changed it out of a strong dislike of the Missouri branch of the Faulkners, and William later changed it back to its first spelling) had been dead eight years when our author, his great-grandson and namesake, was born. He had been properly celebrated by his family, and it was therefore inconceivable that the one Faulkner who had obviously inherited the Colonel's literary talents would ignore him. In *Sartoris, The Unvanquished,* and other novels and stories, the Colonel appears as Colonel John Sartoris, with all of the original Colonel's actual career laid out in faithful detail — the first volunteer regiment in the Civil War, the demotion, the new regiment, the railroad, the encounters with Thurmond, etc. — "colored and modeled, naturally, in the interests of fiction and magnified to heroic proportions, so that Colonel Sartoris becomes the quintessence of his time and class."

Magnified, but not exaggerated, Colonel Falkner was not the typical or conventional Southerner. He had little in common with the plantation aristocracy, was highly skeptical of the grandiose and self-deluding myths by which many of the older Southerners struggled to live, and in his restlessness and willingness to take chances reflected more of the frontier than the delta temperament. If he defended the "Southern way of life," it was with some apparent reluctance, with little ideological conviction, and with a sense of loyalty that he was not ready to reject. "And it may not be too farfetched to suppose," says Irving Howe, "that this mixture of attitudes toward the South was partly inherited by the novelist William Faulkner, in whose work ambivalent feelings toward the homeland would become a major element."

Once the Civil War was over, Colonel Faulkner refused to return to the plantation physically, spiritually, or ideologically. In 1868 he decided to build a railroad that would link

Ripley with the business of the middle South up to Middleton, Tennessee. With the help of a partner, Richard J. Thurmond, a local banker and lawyer, the Ripley Ship Island and Kentucky Railroad was finished, all sixty miles of narrowgauge line. The Colonel was now free to concentrate on his profitable law practice and politics. He helped organize the American Party (better known as the anti-Catholic "Know Nothings") in Mississippi, and moved on to the writing of books. In 1880, he completed *The White Rose of Memphis*, originally serialized in the *Ripley Advertiser*. Although the novel was highly melodramatic and immodestly autobiographical, it became one of the great popular books of its time (160,000 copies, 35 editions, and a modern edition in 1952). *The White Rose* was followed in 1882 by *The Little Brick Church* (all about pre-Revolutionary New York), and in 1884 by *Rapid Ramblings Through Europe*, the Colonel's own vivid account of his impressions and adventures during a trip abroad in 1883.

But writing was merely a hobby with the Colonel; the railroad and politics held first claim on his ambitions. He was by this time a rich man, owned a 1,200-acre plantation, a saw mill, a grist mill, a cotton gin, and assorted small farms. He extended the railroad over Thurmond's objections, ran for the state legislature against Thurmond and won, and soon provoked his former partner to such an extent that Thurmond eventually took out his envy of the Colonel by shooting him. The Colonel died on November 6, 1889. Thurmond was tried for murder, pleaded self-defense, and was acquitted. So ended the saga of Colonel Falkner, a tale that was to provide raw material for many a piece of fiction by his great-grandson, William Faulkner.

EARLY EDUCATION AND READING. Faulkner's early formal education was spotty, his many other preoccupations (especially reading and inventing) taking up so much of his time that he failed to complete high school. After World War I, however, Faulkner was able to enter the University of

Mississippi (1919) under a government-sponsored vocational training program for veterans (a sort of precursor to the more extensive G.I. Bill of Rights program following World War II). In the university, Faulkner shied away from regular courses, taking only those subjects that interested him, especially French. After two or three semesters, he was off to Europe.

It is interesting to note that Faulkner's mother decided that the magazine for him should be *American Boy* (mainly outdoor activities and inventions), for his brother Jack, *Boys' Life,* and for his other brother, John, the more literary *St. Nicholas.* His mother must have started William on Joseph Conrad, Dickens, and probably on *Don Quixote,* as well. In later years he claimed that he annually re-read *Don Quixote,* as well as some Dickens, Balzac, and the *Old Testament.* Shakespeare was not only eminently readable, but definitely portable. William must also have read a great deal of Southern history and books about the Indians. Malcolm Cowley tells us that Faulkner apparently also favored poetry written by or admired by the Symbolists, as well as fiction favored by that school.

INFLUENCE OF STONE. Probably the most serious and effective influence on Faulkner's reading tastes and later literary judgments came from Philip Stone, twenty-one-year-old lawyer with an interest in literature, especially poetry. When Stone was told that the Faulkners' eldest boy showed signs of becoming a poet (William was seventeen at the time), Stone decided to become better acquainted with him. Stone was impressed with the surprisingly good quality of William's poetry, and agreed to become Faulkner's guide, mentor, and arbiter in the realms of reading, literature, and Southern history and culture. The two friends talked about the antebellum South, the Civil War and Reconstruction, decline of the plantation aristocracy along with its outdated value system, Keats and the other Romantic poets. Robert Coughlan maintains that "The picture of the South that he later projected in his stories began to evolve during those long country walks with Stone. Indeed, probably the whole Sartoris conception — and unquestionably the Snopes conception — grew from these conversations which took place over a period of years." The debt to Stone was repaid later when Stone appeared as Gavin Stevens (according to many critics) in several of Faulkner's stories and novels.

FAULKNER JOINS R.A.F. In 1918, Faulkner lost two of his best friends, but only temporarily. Stone went to Yale, and Estelle Oldham, Faulkner's girl friend, married Cornell Franklin. (After her divorce, Faulkner did marry her; and Stone, of course, eventually did return to Oxford and remained Faulkner's lifelong friend and adviser.) The shock was too much for him (he left town before the wedding to take a job in a bookstore near Phil), and he decided to join the Army. He was turned down for being too short; the U.S. Signal Corps also turned him down, despite his experience in flying planes, because he hadn't had two years of college. He was finally accepted by the Royal Canadian Air Force, a branch of the Royal Air Force, and was commissioned a lieutenant. He was back in Oxford before Christmas of that year, fully panoplied in his British uniform, swagger stick, and trench coat. "For the rest of his life," John Faulkner writes, "he wore trench coats. I don't know how many he bought and wore out. It must have run to half a dozen."

FAULKNER IN NEW YORK. After Faulkner left the University in 1920, he wandered around until, at the suggestion of Stark Young, he left for New York in 1923. He stayed there with Young, picked up any odd jobs he could get, and in time was able to get one (through Young) as a clerk in the Doubleday book department in Lord and Taylor's department store. The pay was $11 a week, his room rent was $2.50 a week. But the department was managed by Elizabeth Prall (later to marry Sherwood Anderson), and merely establishing a *literary* connection with her was worth the drabness of the whole New York experience. After six months of vain efforts trying to impress publishers, Faulkner was happy to hear from Stone that he could have the University post-mastership, if he wanted it.

FAULKNER AS POSTMASTER. Faulkner always wanted to be a "man of letters," but the postmaster's job was not exactly what he had meant. The job was dull, mail piled up, students and professors found it difficult to keep up with the vagaries of Faulkner's schedule, records were lost or ignored, and customers began complaining about other things only distantly related to the operation of a post office — such as Faulkner's long walks (often barefoot), his writing of poetry, and his drinking. One of the town's ministers even preached from his pulpit against Faulkner and his drinking. "Bill never did do as much drinking as he got credit for," his brother John writes. "He never tried to hide it but he did do most of it at home. . . . But people talk and their stories grow and that's the way it was about Bill's drinking."

Stone tried to cover up for Faulkner as long as he could, but finally Faulkner had to yield to popular opinion and quit (John Faulkner claims his brother was fired). Soon after his "liberation" from the post office, Faulkner began writing in earnest. His first book, a collection of poems entitled *The Marble Faun,* was published with money put up by Phil Stone. Of the 1,000 copies printed, about 50 were sold. The rest Phil stored in his own home.

FAULKNER IN NEW ORLEANS. In 1925, Stone came up with yet another idea for promoting the career of his protege. Why not go abroad and make your reputation as a poet there, as did T. S. Eliot, Ezra Pound, and others? In January, the two friends went to New Orleans, Stone for a vacation, Faulkner to find a berth (in exchange for work) on any ship bound for Europe. The job never developed, Stone returned to Mississippi, and Faulkner remained in New Orleans completely at loose ends. One day by luck Faulkner learned that his old boss from New York days, Elizabeth

Prall, was in town with her newly acquired husband, Sherwood Anderson. Faulkner called on her and was introduced to Anderson, a writer whom he admired. The friendship between Faulkner and Anderson grew even as Faulkner began writing his first novel, *Soldier's Pay,* under the influence of the Bohemian group over which Anderson presided and of the rich, carefree life that Anderson was able to lead as a writer. If this was what a writer's life could be, then he, Faulkner, wanted to be a writer, too.

NOVELIST AT LAST. When the manuscript of *Soldier's Pay* was completed, Elizabeth Prall Anderson agreed to give it to her husband, but she did not promise that he would read it, and he didn't. But Sherwood Anderson did tell his publisher, Horace Liveright, on his arrival in New Orleans, of his "discovery." Liveright read the manuscript and agreed to publish it. Now Faulkner could join all the other writers, would-be writers, and artists in the French Quarter of which Sherwood Anderson might have been characterized in the (later) Faulknerian phrase as "sole owner and proprietor." With his credentials as a writer now duly certified, Faulkner contributed to the group's official journal, *The Double Dealer* (Hemingway joined Faulkner in the June number with a poem entitled "Ultimately"), and sold some short stories to the New Orleans *Times-Picayune,* which thus acquired the enviable distinction of being the first publication of any kind to publish his fiction. Most of his second novel, *Mosquitoes,* was also written during his stay in New Orleans. On the basis of Faulkner's ultimate position in American literature, one must judge both *Mosquitoes* and *Soldier's Pay* potboilers. In any event, both novels were strongly derivative of Hemingway, Dos Passos, and Aldous Huxley, even though the subject matter was authentic and culled strictly from Faulkner's own experiences.

FAREWELL TO ANDERSON. Everything was now going well with Faulkner, especially his connections with Anderson and the Anderson group. But then Faulkner decided to collaborate with William Spratling on a book called *Sherwood Anderson and Other Famous Creoles*. Spratling would do the drawings, Faulkner the text. So far, so good. Then Faulkner decided that it would be very appropriate if he could write the introduction to the book in Anderson's own literary style. Although no malice was intended, Anderson could not see the humor in what he construed as a cruel parody (Hemingway had also parodied him in *The Torrents of Spring*, a takeoff on his own *Dark Laughter*) and abruptly terminated their friendship.

1929 — A VERY GOOD YEAR. This was the year in which Faulkner saw *Sartoris* (the first Yoknapatawpha novel) and *The Sound and The Fury* (still considered the best of all his novels) published, began writing *As I Lay Dying*, married Estelle Oldham Franklin, and purchased Rowan Oak. Faulkner had been turned down once when Estelle Oldham, his childhood sweetheart, accepted her family's suggestion in 1918 that she marry the more reliable lawyer, Cornell Franklin, rather than the bohemian would-be writer, Faulkner. In 1927 she divorced Franklin and returned to Oxford with her two children. This time Faulkner was much more acceptable, and the marriage took place two years later. Now Faulkner laid down the first lines of the country-squire pattern he was to follow for the rest of his life. When a dilapidated colonial mansion, Rowan Oak, that once belonged to an Irish planter, became available, Faulkner bought it and started putting enormous sums of money into restoring it to its former baronial grandeur. The house, the only one Faulkner ever owned in Oxford, came with fourteen acres, but he added some more of the land adjacent to it, installed electricity and hot water, and eventually added more rooms, a back parlor, and another bathroom or two. It was from this ante-bellum, two-storied house with columns across the center section in front that Faulkner was buried in 1962.

FAULKNER IN HOLLYWOOD: PHASE ONE. With the publication of *Sanctuary* in 1931, Faulkner emerged as a fairly popular writer. This American Gothic tale of terror, sex, and perversion convinced Hollywood that Faulkner's novels might be the stuff of which successful "X-rated" films could be made. (There was of course no such rating at the time, but Hollywood did have a kind of "Condemned" rating which *Sanctuary* as a film just managed to evade.) Faulkner was called out to the Coast to help adapt the novel for the screen under the title of *The Story of Temple Drake*. After completing that assignment for Howard Hawks, Faulkner worked on several other literary properties, his own and others'. Hawks considered him a writer who had "inventiveness, taste, and great ability to characterize and the visual imagination to translate these qualities into the medium of the screen. He is intelligent and obliging — a master of his work who does it without fuss. . . ." (as reported by Robert Coughlan). Faulkner returned to Hollywood in 1935 and again in 1942 to pick up extra money that he sorely needed in order to live in the style to which he had become accustomed. Rowan Oak alone became a visible monument to the many hours he had put into writing Hollywood scripts.

FAULKNER BUYS FARM. Faulkner turned down many invitations, including one from the late President John F. Kennedy, on the pretext that as a working farmer he could not spare the time away from his crops or his livestock. In 1938, he had purchased a farm and let it out to be run by three Black tenant families (a total of five working hands). They were permitted to keep the profits, if any, in accordance with Faulkner's belief that "The Negroes don't always get a square deal in Mississippi." That might be one explanation for this quixotic scheme. Another might be that this was Faulkner's way of returning to the land, a theme that recurs throughout most of his works. Still another might be that this was Faulkner's way of mitigating the "curse" that fell upon the South when the land was taken from the original Indian settlers. Whatever the explanation, the fact remained that beef produced on that farm cost Faulkner five dollars a pound.

A MAJOR WRITER RECOGNIZED. By 1939, Faulkner had produced ten novels, two volumes of poetry, and two collections of short stories. The public had refused to recognize him as a major writer except for *Sanctuary*. But the critics and Faulkner's peers were taking notice of his considerable body of works, and it was they who started the long list of honors which follows:

1939—Elected to National Institute of Arts and Letters
1948—Elected to American Academy of Arts and Letters
1950—Received William Dean Howells Medal for Fiction
        Awarded Nobel Prize for Literature
1955—Received National Book Award
        Awarded Pulitzer Prize for Literature (Fiction)

FURTHER RECOGNITION. Once Faulkner's credentials as a writer were established, the next step was to recognize him *as an authority* on writing. The latter recognition came in such forms as:

1954—Attendance at the International Writer's Conference, Sao Paulo, Brazil
1955—Attendance at the Writer's Seminar at Nagano, Japan
1957—Appointment as Writer-in-Residence, University of Virginia
1958—Reappointment as Writer-in-Residence, University of Virginia

Faulkner was now also recognized as a multifaceted celebrity. In 1955, he made two trips abroad for the U.S. State Department. In 1956, articles by him on integration appeared in *Life, Harper's,* and *Ebony* magazine. Stage productions of *Requiem for a Nun* were given in Paris (1956) and Greece (1957). In 1962, he was invited to the White

House (along with other Nobel laureates), and turned down the invitation. Three months later, Faulkner was dead (July 6) in Oxford.

FAULKNER AND THE SOUTHERN MYTH. Myth is usually defined as a story or legend or collection of stories or legends that relate in thinly allegorical form the most basic experiences of a people. The Southern myth (or any other myth) does not attempt to report with any historical accuracy either the collective imagination or the collective will. The reader can find perhaps the simplest expression of the Southern myth in the collection of Civil War stories called *The Unvanquished* (Faukner insisted this work was a novel). In much more sophisticated form, it appears in *Absalom, Absalom!*, a novel which Irving Howe believes Faulkner wrote "out of sheer pain, in which Faulkner forced himself to see how the will to domination had corrupted the white community. Between these two extremes lies the bulk of his major fiction."

Howe goes so far as to say that Faulkner's "agony," ambivalence over the Southern myth, frequently manifests itself in his "tortured, forced, and even incoherent" language, mainly because Faulkner "worked with the decayed fragments of a myth, the soured pieties of regional memory. . . ." Faulkner could accept the present, not with equanimity or logic, but with hopelessness and despair; whatever pride he had was rooted in the past. He was fully aware of the tension (of every sort) that existed between the past and the present (Sartre maintained that for Faulkner — and for many of his characters — the future did not exist at all), and try as he would Faulkner could not accept the Southern myth in its entirety, even if it meant a kind of illusionary, inward peace. The relation between the Southern tradition, which he admired to some extent, and the bitter memory of Southern slavery, to which he felt forced to return, caused him much wonderment and confusion. From time to time he measured the present against the past, and likewise the past against the myth, and eventually the myth itself against moral absolutes. "This testing of the myth," says Howe, "though by no means the only important activity in Faulkner's work, is basic to the Yoknapatawpha novels and stories."

FAULKNER AS SOUTHERN TRADITIONALIST. Some critics have maintained that Faulkner, stripped of all his literary ambitions, devices, and obfuscations, is a Southern traditionalist, a conservative moralist, deriving his creative strength from an almost umbilical attachment to the Southern past. Cowley describes Faulkner's social view as that of an "anti-slavery nationalist." George M. O'Donnell insists that Faulkner is a traditional moralist who persistently defends the "Southern socio-economic-ethical tradition." Howe finds a middle position for Faulkner: "His work contains a wide range of attitudes toward the South, from sentimentality to denunciation, from identification to rejection." Edmund Wilson sees in Faulkner a romantic morality based on the chivalry which was a valid part of the Southern heritage. From the earlier works on (at least after *Pylon*), Wilson detects a sort of romantic morality that "allows you the thrills of melodrama without making you ashamed, as a rule, of the values which have been invoked to produce them." Why fault Faulkner, Wilson asks, for his persistent identification with the mentality of his homeland? To Wilson, this loyalty or chivalry *is* Faulkner's morality, a vital part of his Southern heritage. Furthermore, this morality, Wilson contends, is a force "more humane and more positive than almost anything one can find in the work of even those writers of our more mechanized societies who have set out to defend human rights."

Be that as it may, for O'Donnell, Faulkner is a traditionalist in a modern, emerging South. "All around him the anti-traditional forces are at work, and he lives among evidences of their past activity," O'Donnell writes. "He could not fail to be aware of them. It is not strange, then, that his novels are primarily a series of related myths (or aspects of a single myth) built around the conflict between traditionalism and the antitraditional modern world in which it is immersed."

FAULKNER'S VISION OF HUMAN LIFE. With the publication of *Sanctuary* in 1931, Faulkner's outlook on life became decidedly more negative. This is not to say that he was ever completely free of misanthropy and despair in the earlier novels; but *Sanctuary* marked a definite change from the "troubled but tender and intensely human world" of *The Sound and The Fury* to the perverse and the pathological. In exchanging the innocence of Benjy for the corrupt and perverted Popeye, Faulkner was in essence denying humanity. Indeed, he was still describing the world of childhood (says Maxwell Geismar), but now a very depressingly different aspect of it: "the world of human perversions whose precise nature is that they also are infantile emotions; they are the reflections of our early animal instincts which have been blocked and forced out of their formal channels of maturing." The loss of innocence so tenderly mourned in *The Sound and The Fury* became in his later novels the subject of repeated and strident attacks on man's understandable penchant for behaving a little worse than the angels.

And yet, wasn't Faulkner's *human and artistic* progression from the Compsons to the Snopes, from Benjy to Popeye, from Caddy to Temple Drake and Eula Varner a very natural and expected one? Faulkner, like Shakespeare (from the early happy comedies to the "dark and bitter" comedies later on, for example) and other significant writers, had to seek out a serious and mature vision of life, one that, says Howe, "could include both moral criticism and pleasure in sensuous experience, a vision that accepts both the power of fate, all that binds and breaks us, and the possibility of freedom, all that permits us to shape our being."

FAULKNER, HONOR, AND INTEGRITY. Perhaps because Faulkner was born and bred in the South, we expect. him to be preoccupied with the concept of honor. It is frequently operative in his novels, especially the earlier ones, but it is a "strangely elusive concept — more a cry than a substance — and increasingly cut off from moral issues." In his later novels and stories, Faulkner came to think more about integrity than honor. Honor concerns itself with what we are in the world, with pride and dignity, status and reputation, all that is external, like a mask; integrity concerns itself with the inner man, his ease of being and his ease of conscience. For such a change in emphasis, Faulkner must be commended, because it carried him to an ever-expanding humaneness and thoughtfulness, to a depth of feeling far beyond the superficialities of human behavior. As Faulkner perceived it, integrity is accessible to *every* kind of human being in *any* social stratum and in *any* kind of situation. *(The whites he perceived as more concerned with the preservation of their honor, the Blacks more often concerned with the preservation of their integrity.)* For his artistic and moral purposes, he chose to exploit the more extreme situations, mainly because he wished to test all that was "intractable" and "indomitable" in human character under the most compelling pressures.

FAULKNER'S PHILOSOPHY SUMMARIZED. As Howe sees it, the artistic and moral pattern of all of Faulkner's works is made up of a series of strands or biases: his respect before suffering, his contempt for deceit, his belief in the rightness of self-trust, and his enlarging compassion for the defeated. Of all of these, the last he considered the most significant. True heroism implied exposure, taking a chance, resisting everything that comes between birth and death, plunging into the depths of experience to extend one's range of consciousness, fighting against one's *predestined* (by fate, theology, etc.) or *conditioned* (by society, circumstances, etc.) niche in life. Through resistance, Faulkner felt, came freedom.

# WILLIAM FAULKNER, "SOLE OWNER AND PROPRIETOR" OF YOKNAPATAWPHA COUNTY

IN SEARCH OF A SUBJECT. Even after he had completed his first two novels, *Soldier's Pay* and *Mosquitoes*, Faulkner was still a writer without a subject. He could have settled for being a *general* storyteller, jumping from one popular or marketable subject to another, but such a career did not suit his temperament. The compulsion within him was too strong to resist; he needed, as Irving Howe points out, "some organizing principle in experience and a subject by which to release it in his writing." And once he discovered this subject — or did it discover him, for it must have been lying dormant in his deepest memories? — he stuck with it through fifteen of his nineteen novels. For Faulkner the writer, as for Faulkner the private man, the South — Southern memory, Southern reality, Southern myth — became the "special world." And basic to this "special world" would be the defeat of the homeland, a process that began long before the Civil War itself. Faulkner would struggle long and sincerely to forestall the ultimate end, sometimes through romanticizing the truth (i.e., by enhancing the myth) as in some parts of *Sartoris*, or by evoking sympathy of the reader through the hopeless picture of social loss, as in *The Sound and The Fury*.

FAULKNERS AND SARTORISES. Once the skeleton of the subject had been identified, Faulkner proceeded to flesh it out. For Oxford, read Jefferson; for Lafayette County, read Yoknapatawpha County, and for the Faulkners, read the Sartorises. (We shall deal with the Sartorises first; Yoknapatawpha County will be treated at greater length below.) The Sartoris family appears "full time" in one novel and one volume of short stories, and plays leading or supporting parts in many of the other books. Their glories and agonies are the glories and agonies of the Faulkners, but seen from William Faulkner's point of view and "adjusted" by him to accommodate the needs of fiction. There is nothing reprehensible in this process, nor does the author have to acknowledge or reject any of the so-called autobiographical elements.

In *Sartoris*, the first of Faulkner's novels about the decadent Sartoris and Compson families of Jefferson in Yoknapatawpha County, the author began reciting the long, sad saga of the decay of the genteel society of the old Civil War South, later to be replaced during the years following World War I by the more realistic, pragmatic, worldly, unscrupulous Snopeses. As early as *The Sound and The Fury*, we are made aware of the "manifest destiny" of the Snopeses through the limited dealings that Jason Compson has with them. He, moreover, has already become less of a Compson and more like a Snopes, an omen of things to come.

Whether he calls the families Sartoris or Compson or De Spain, Faulkner in many of his books is concerned with the losing fight these good, noble and brave leaders of the old South were waging against the Snopeses. Nor is he trying to defend them as the "good guys" against the "bad guys." He is well aware of the fact that it was they who introduced slavery into the South, a sin that must be expiated until the final takeover by the Snopeses.

THEORY OF HUMAN EROSION. According to Faulkner, then, the best form of expiation for that major sin is the punishment the land itself has imposed on the Sartorises. It was slavery that put a curse on the land, and the land in turn put a curse on the Sartorises. Until that curse can be lifted by generations of individual expiation, the "legal fiction" (Faulkner's own term) is shifting to the Snopeses. They, for their part, even as they exploit the land to its uttermost limits of physical exhaustion, themselves become hol-

low, impotent men and women. They, too, will be defeated in
the long run, Faulkner believes, and the land itself will
emerge as the hero, God, and major protagonist — at least
in his novels. We may therefore be dealing here with a new
philosophy, *Geophily,* or the wild, mystical love of the land,
expressed more simply and dramatically by one of the characters in *Sanctuary:* "People don't own land. It's the land
that owns the people."

Then there is always the possibility that Faulkner was a
visionary who foresaw the time when we would become concerned with the way in which man, *all* men, was plundering
the earth and the very planet itself. Was Faulkner then a
mystical ecologist, or an ecological mystic? But that would
be an oversimplification. For Faulkner the ultimate disaster
was *human* erosion.

FAULKNER'S SOUTH. How shall we describe this land,
this South, that ruins the people it nourishes? Faulkner
himself came very close in his picture of *his* part of the
South, a land so "surrealistic and monotonous in its flatness
that it appears unnatural, even menacing."

Edith Hamilton feels that Faulkner's novels are about
"ugly people in an ugly land." She finds no beauty anywhere
in his novels, and whether he deliberately excluded it or did
not perceive it, she cannot say. But it was the land that was
the more unbeautiful of the two. A dark curse lay on it; as
Faulkner says, it was "already tainted before any white
man owned it . . . from that old world's corrupt and worthless twilight as though in the sailfulls of the old world's
tainted wind which drove the ships [Columbus's, Faulkner
presumably meant]." The initial curse, then, must have been
connected with the dispossession of the Indians, first by
Columbus and then by the English, both in the North and in
the South. The South, however, according to Faulkner, had
to assume the major consequences of the curse. In *The Bear,*
for example, it is young Ike McCaslin who defines the curse

best: "Don't you see? Don't you see? This whole land, the whole South, is cursed, and all of us who derive from it, whom it ever suckled, lie under the curse."

*THE BEAR.* The major part of Faulkner's *Go Down, Moses* is the novelette entitled *The Bear,* perhaps Faulkner's most perfect piece of sustained writing. Aside from its very obvious literary excellences, it is the story of a hunt and at the same time, a *symbolic fable* about the entrance into manhood and moral responsibility of a young boy, Isaac McCaslin. It may also prove, upon further analysis, to be what Irving Howe has called the "centerpiece of Faulkner's entire work." Every year the men of Yoknapatawpha go off on their ritual visit to the forest; *ritual* because the purpose is "not to hunt bear and deer but to keep the yearly rendezvous with the bear which they did not even intend to kill." This year Isaac McCaslin is considered old enough to join the men in their "religious retreat" from money, the town and its social stratification, women, etc. (Echoes reverberate herein of Shakespeare's *Love's Labor's Lost.*) Assigned to assist the sixteen-year-old Isaac in his "initiation" is Sam Fathers, the "taintless and incorruptible" old man of mixed Negro and Indian blood who is also the acknowledged authority on the "priestly" rites that will be performed in the forest.

Before Isaac can meet the bear, he must strip himself of all social and material possessions, especially his watch and compass, so that he can — and must — rely on sun and stars and other natural "aids." When he does see the bear, he is seized with an "ecstasy of communion," and is properly "inspired" to refuse to kill the animal. Not animal so much as *totem* and *symbol* of the unspoken bond with nature that joins the hunters together and will be dissolved if the animal is killed. But the hunters are realistic enough to know that sooner or later that bond will be destroyed as the bear is destroyed, because that is the inevitable end of the historic process through which they are all going at that very moment. Their one hope is that Isaac will truly persevere, despite the inevitable, to preserve the memory of the bear, the meaning of the "pageant-rite," and the more commendable values of the fraternity of the hunters. Following this first "communion" and "confirmation" combined, Isaac will go back to the town and there, by refusing to accept his heritage (the curse of the land) and by deciding to live simply and poorly, will "perhaps break the chain of guilt binding him to the communal past."

The idea of a pastoral retreat to "the Eden of the wilderness" did not appear first in *The Bear*; it can be found in a less clearly articulated form in the character of the idiot Benjy, a natural innocent, and in the romantic Puritan (and puritan), Quentin, both in *The Sound and The Fury*. Nor is the idea at all original with Faulkner. Mention has already been made of Shakespeare's extremely romantic gestures toward the return to the simplicities of nature, in both *Love's Labor's Lost* and *As You Like It*. Faulkner must of course have been impressed by the "rhythmic harmonies of the natural world, in contrast to the frenzy and corruption of social life" during those recurrent hunting trips with his father back in Oxford. Also, very likely, through his readings in Mark Twain (especially *Huckleberry Finn*), in Herman Melville (the sea has here replaced the forest), and in the Leatherstocking novels of James Fenimore Cooper.

"The myth of a natural return is a myth of space, possible only to a people for whom the land once seemed to stretch out endlessly. . . . It is a recalling [of] a time when men could measure their independence by their distance from each other," says Howe. For Faulkner and for those other American writers (including Hemingway), it was the wilderness, unviolated nature, that was the scene of nobility (c.f. Rousseau's "noble savage"), freedom, and, above all, innocence. Society, according to both these writers and our modern ecologists, began to suffocate these values even as it began to suffocate the earth itself.

YOKNAPATAWPHA COUNTY. Yoknapatawpha County is 2,400 square miles in area. It is bounded by the Talahatchie and Yoknapatawpha rivers. It comprises mainly farmlands and pine hills. According to the census (Faulkner's), there are in the county 15,611 inhabitants, 6,298 white and 9,313 Negro. It is a land blighted by poverty and scarcity of indus-trialization. There are no distinct social classes, but clans reflecting family pride and reverence for ancestors. Its main town is Jefferson, and not too far away from Jefferson is Mattson.

Yoknapatawpha County compares roughly with Lafayette County, Mississippi.

"Faulkner abhors the reasonable mind which neatly con-structs and resolves its work. Since he cannot free himself entirely of his familiar world," Rabi says, "Faulkner tries to recreate it in his imagination. We can therefore think of a Faulknerian geography and a Faulknerian climate, a fixed element in which his people move. Jefferson appears per-sistently at the center of his map."

Of all his novels, only *Soldier's Pay, Mosquitoes, Pylon* and *A Fable* fall outside the Yoknapatawpha complex. One must therefore wonder, once Faulkner felt the need to create an imaginary locale for most of his works (a locale, by the way, which he believed in so strongly that he even drew a map of the area for the 1946 *Portable Faulkner* collection of his works), where did he find the raw data for his very own property? Lafayette County was established in 1836. It is a 679-square-mile section of Mississippi of pine-covered hills, bounded on the north by the Talahatchie River and on the south by the Yocnany River (in those times, however, it was called the "Yocanapatafa," close enough to Faulkner's own choice of county name, *Yoknapatawpha*). Within four years, the population reached 3,689 whites and 2,842 Negro slaves. After the Treaty of Pontotoc, by which the resident Indians agreed to move to the new Oklahoma Territory, a handful of Indians chose to remain in Lafayette.

When Faulkner speaks of Jefferson, he is also speaking of Oxford; when he speaks of Yoknapatawpha, he is also speaking of Lafayette. Faulkner essentially never strays far from the historical or factual past. There were real clans in Lafayette just as there were the fictional clans of Compsons, Sartorises, and McCaslins. Both types of clans were beginning to break up during the period between the 1890's and late 1930's covered by most of the Yoknapatawpha books, as the traditional Southern life style found it increasingly more difficult to resist change. The fictional clans reacted to the inroads of modernism in Yoknapatawpha in a variety of ways. The Sartorises came to symbolize a chivalric recklessness and self-destruction. The Compsons came to stand for a more extreme and tragic disintegration. The McCaslins, the South's last best hope, fought back with an heroic effort to atone for the evil of the past. And opposed to these representatives of a dying South was the Snopes clan, on a decidedly lower level, the "sourceless" flotsam (the adjective is Faulkner's) ready to move in and fill the vacuum once the older classes begin to disintegrate and secede from the social scene itself. Whether rootlessness, as represented by the Snopeses, was the major cause of the disintegration of traditional Southern society, or whether inherent weaknesses and contradictions of the Southern tradition were the cause, is a moot question. Even Faulkner, whether within the fictional or the factual context, is ambivalent about the cause; hence, the moot question.

**YOKNAPATAWPHA, FAULKNER, AND BALZAC.** Comparison has often been made between the Yoknapatawpha series of novels and the novels of Balzac covering the "Human Condition." In respect to the scope of the work, Faulkner can be compared with Balzac. If Balzac's literary "turf" was the France of his era treated in every minute detail as a social panorama, Faulkner's world, his "own little postage stamp of native soil," was no less complex. Its dimensions might have been smaller, but, as Faulkner himself said, "I would never live long enough to exhaust it, and that by sublimating the actual into the apocryphal I would have complete liberty to use whatever talent I might have to its absolute top." Which brings us to the main difference between Faulkner and Balzac — treatment of the material.

Balzac may be said to have created a "tapestry" in which every scene or thread had a planned relationship to every other. But Faulkner (recalling Rabi's apt comment), "abhors a reasonable mind which neatly constructs and resolves its work," and thus applies the method of "collage" rather than "tapestry" to assemble many diverse and often seemingly disparate elements, brought together by intuition more than by deliberate, artistic intent. One device employed by Faulkner to bring into unity seemingly disjointed and unrelated elements is his manipulation of time. Unlike Balzac, he is no slave to chronological time, and is therefore free of the *logic* of chronological time.

Again, unlike Balzac, Faulkner probably never set out to write a series of interrelated books. It was only after he had completed many stories and several novels that he began to be aware of the fact that what he was writing was, essentially, *one* book, the *Yoknapatawpha* book. In a similar circumstance, Balzac might have taken such a realization of artistic direction to draw up a master plan to be followed to the conclusion of the series (as did C. P. Snow in more recent times with his eleven-volume *Strangers and Brothers* series). But not Faulkner; still trusting to his intuition, he continued writing as and what he pleased. The "collage" kept growing as Faulkner kept moving back and forth in time to create related episodes to serve as prologues or sequels to stories and novels already completed. As Faulkner told Malcolm Cowley (in explaining the dual nature of the Appendix to *The Sound and The Fury* almost twenty years after the book was first published — the Compsons *before* 1928 and the Compsons *after* 1928, the novel itself covering three days in 1928 and one day in 1910 in the life of the Compsons), no book of his was every really finished. "It has been a method eclectic, pragmatic, intensely private, and essentially poetic," writes Robert Coughlan. It has also been a method similar to that used by a casting director in a theatrical stock company — casting and recasting characters or actors in major and minor roles interchangeably to meet the needs of the current script. Thus, Quentin Compson has a "star" role in *The Sound and The Fury*, but only a "supporting" role in *Absalom, Absalom!*

YOKNAPATAWPHA: PROVINCIAL OR UNIVERSAL? There is some doubt among critics that Yoknapatawpha is that distinct and unique a place. Sean O'Faolain, the Irish writer, sees the same provincialism in Yoknapatawpha that he sees in County Cork, the same local patriotism, and the same Southern (Southern Irish or Southern American) nationalism. "There is the same vanity of an old race; the same gnawing sense of old defeat; the same capacity for intense hatred; a good deal of the same harsh folk-humor; the same acidity; the same oscillation between unbounded self-confidence and total despair; the same escape through sport and drink." But Cleanth Brooks observes that even though an Irishman can recognize at once the similarities between the two provincialisms, O'Faolain "manages to misunderstand the use that Faulkner makes of his." And therein lies the difference, the difference that makes Faulkner not only the "sole owner and proprietor" of Yoknapatawpha County, but also its sole authority and interpreter.

FAULKNER AS EXPERIMENTAL NOVELIST. Faulkner could have been a first-rank, traditional storyteller, had he chosen to stick to the "linear" pattern of events proceeding from a specific, precise beginning to a specific, precise end. Such a technique is clearly evident in most of his short stories (he was probably basically a short-story writer) and in many of his novels. Even in *The Sound and The Fury*, his most experimental novel, the reader finds little difficulty in following the narrative flow as early as the beginning of the third or Jason section.

Faulkner chose to experiment with different narrative techniques and other devices probably because he was living during a period in American literature when many of our better writers were beginning to respond to the "experiments" of Proust, Joyce, and Woolf, and because he wished to draw the reader into a more direct commitment to the characters and events in the story, "to saturate him," says Irving Howe, "in the atmospheres of an imagined world, to force him to abandon the posture of a passive listener and become an active participant struggling, like some of Faulkner's characters themselves, to discover meaning in the represented events."

To achieve this conversion of the reader from passivity to active participation and involvement in the story, Faulkner called upon many devices and methods — the stream of consciousness and interior monologues (Joyce, Woolf, Proust), multiple narrators, juggling of time sequences, a convoluted style (Henry James), etc. — and a different approach from one book to another. In *The Sound and The Fury*, he used "free association" with Benjy and Quentin, and the interior monologue with Jason. With Dilsey, he was back to the relatively simple "linear" form of telling a story. *As I Lay Dying* has sometimes been referred to as a "cantata for fifteen voices" or "variations (fifteen of them) on a theme," there being fifteen characters each speaking his or her own piece for a total of sixty narrative and reflective phrases or fragments. *Light in August* is essentially a straight, naturalistic novel, with emphasis (somewhat in the manner of John Dos Passos) on detail after detail. In *Absalom, Absalom!*, Faulkner reverted to a considerable extent to the elements of the Gothic romance. In *The Hamlet* and *The Reivers*, Faulkner turned back to the commendable tradition of the American tall tale or "whopper." *Go Down, Moses* is a collection of loosely connected (not by *leitmotifs* but by common characters), sprawling tales, with *The Bear* the most memorable tale in the whole collection. The reader can see in *The Wild Palms* two distinct narratives, one alternating with the other until one has taken on meaning from the other — a dialogue, as it were, between two stories. *Requiem for a Nun* is, with little doubt, Faulkner's attempt to write dramatic prose (cf. Henry James as dramatist manqué). The novel is clearly divided into acts as in a play, with "elegiac prose rhapsodies about the Yoknapatawpha past" interposing. *Intruder in the Dust* is basically a darn good "whodunit." And *A Fable,* finally, is Faulkner's less-than-successful attempt at writing contrived allegory. As one critic put it, "When Faulkner was trying, he was very, very *trying.*" *But in the last analysis, it is this very fact, namely, that Faulkner was at all times experimenting with the novel form, that makes Faulkner unforgettable.*

SOURCES OF FAULKNER'S STYLE. Faulkner was a natural genius in the authentic American tradition — untutored (or self-tutored), undisciplined (or self-disciplined), unbuttoned and informal, erratic, extravagant, and sometimes vulgar (that is, earthy, of the people). But it was the drive of his genius that compelled him to resort to the more open, relaxed forms of storytelling rather than to the more rigid, more easily recognizable ones. The content he chose dictated the form he was to choose: myths and legends drawn from the "collective memory of his homeland" did not fit too easily into the prescribed molds of fiction. Like Shakespeare, he found it easier and more natural to plunge into the dramatic scene, to let the words and images flow in torrents, if need be, in oratorical or declamatory style, in wild comedy or extreme melodrama. Edmund Wilson found in Faulkner's earlier novels echoes of Hemingway and Sherwood Anderson. But the more consistent and persistent echoes were to be found, said Wilson, in the "full-dress post-Flaubert group of Conrad, Joyce and Proust." Faulkner may have started with their kind of highly complex fiction, but he then added to it the "rich and lively resources, reappearing with amazing freshness, of English lyric verse and romantic prose (as distinguished from what we now call American)." This gift, which Faullkner shared with other

Southern writers, is made possible (Wilson concludes) by
"a contact with the language of Shakespeare which, if they
sidestep the oratorical Southern verbiage, they may get
through their old-fashioned education." And through a contact with the language of the Bible, which shares with Shakespeare the many excellences of Elizabethan and Jacobean
English.

FAULKNER'S PROSE. But Faulkner did not always manage to "sidestep the oratorical Southern verbiage." In fact,
says Edmund Volpe, "Had Faulkner been a U.S. senator, his
speeches would have been squarely in the tradition of Southern oratory. Some of his sentences sound almost like selected
passages from a filibuster . . ." Volpe believes that the touch-
stone for evaluating or describing Faulkner's prose, its syntax and diction, the structure of its sentences, its vocabulary,
its total texture, in short, is to be found in oratory. Other
less friendly critics have described Faulkner's prose as:
*ambiguous, eccentric, over-elaborate, bizarre, surrealistic,
precious, romantic, archaic, lyrical, baroque, incantatory,
hypnotic, turgid, garrulous, compulsive,* and *lush.* Let's consider *oratorical* for our present purposes.

ORATORICAL PROSE. The oral tradition is unquestionably older than the written one. Faulkner not only believed
this, but *he often seemed to be writing down something he
was listening to,* a voice narrating an old Southern myth or
legend, or a recent bit of local gossip. Many of his stories
and novels, therefore, may very well be actual oral narra-
tions. Had he lived longer into the electronic age *as an active
writer,* Faulkner might have chosen to do what many of our
current writers (especially the non-fiction ones) do — take
down the actual oral narration on tape and then transcribe
(or transmute, depending on the energy and literary talent
of the "listener") it as prose literature. Very often, Faulkner's prose sounds like an actual recording of a non-stop
talker, or what Volpe calls "talk-prose."

SYNTAX AND DICTION. If we accept this premise, it is easier to pick out the predominant characteristics of *spoken* prose that pervade (and often overpower) Faulkner's written prose. In spoken prose, the complete sentence as a self-contained unit of thought is far less important or necessary than it is in written prose. A grunt, a phrase, an expletive or interjection (with appropriate gesture or facial expression) can often convey more meaning than the longest of Faulkner's (or Henry James's) sentences. Much conversation, even among educated, cultured and literate people, would defy (traditional or prescriptive) syntactical analysis. Hence the continuing disagreements between speech-centered and grammar-centered instructors in our liberal-arts institutions. Faulkner may also have been closer to the original meaning of the term "rhetoric," that is, a system of techniques, devices, and rules for *oral* expression or oratory. Thus, he makes use of the rhetorical devices of oratory (a redundancy herein), building his sentences with parallel units or "layers" of nouns, or verbals, or phrases, or clauses with their modifiers set in parallel construction. Balancing or juxtaposing of opposites, negatives against positives, for example, is also right out of the rhetoric handbook.

CASCADING NOUNS AND ADJECTIVES. Almost every one of the common nouns in a Faulkner sentence has at least one adjective to modify it. In rare instances, Faulkner will revert to the more economical style of poetry to create a sharp image with a few simple, even familiar, words. More frequently he will rely upon qualifying phrases, clauses, compounded or massed adjectives, to express a nuance of thought or feeling. In some of his novels, particularly the later ones, the linguistic cascade roars apace — noun upon noun, adjective upon adjective, impatient phrase upon phrase. The syntax then becomes a hopeless tangle, a "thickly matted jungle of clauses and phrases, defying, by clear intention, the schoolbook rules of grammar."

SENTENCES. A critic once referred to Faulkner's sentences

as "uncommutable life sentences." But it is not just the length of them that the attentive reader soon becomes aware of; the torturing of some of his sentences and the violent wrenching of some of his words, crowding into a unit of language more than it seems possible for it to bear (the old grammatical term for a sentence was *clausus*, literally a closed unit with specific limits and dimensions), occurred not because Faulkner was *un-* or *anti*-grammatical, or that he was indifferent to the need for clarity, but that he was trying to squeeze into one sentence the "sense of simultaneity . . . the sense of the palpitating complexity of felt experience."

Be that as it may, Faulkner's sentences take on their convoluted or viscous quality through a very conscious method of placing modifying elements after the noun, as in poetry (and let us not forget, Faulkner was a poet first, a novelist later). With the usual word order inverted (as in German, for example), he could keep adding modifier after modifier, afterthought after afterthought, not only with adjectives, but also with nouns and verbs; and not lithe, slim nouns and verbs, but compounded ones, and masses of them. Volpe calls this invention "free-wheeling."

LOGOPHILIA, OR LOVE OF WORDS. Still another critic referred to Faulkner as a "verbal voluptuary," a man with a lust for language, with an insatiable need for words. When he had seemingly exhausted the available supply of Anglo-Saxon and Latin derivatives (and these included many old words that Faulkner had "resurrected"), he didn't hesitate to coin new words by joining two familiar words into one (as James Joyce and Gerard Manley Hopkins had done before him), or by compounding two words into one through a hyphen. At times, the dictionary or denotative meaning of a word did not serve his purpose, and then he took the connotative or affective meaning instead, again reflecting more of the manner of a poet than a novelist. The end result, Volpe points out, is that Faulkner sometimes sounds stuffy, stilted, and pretentious, "like a self-educated man proudly using the esoteric synonym in place of the one in common usage."

John Faulkner quotes his brother as claiming that the English language just didn't have enough words in it to serve his purposes. "He certainly used just about every one there was," John writes, "and sometimes some most of us didn't even know we had. Every now and then I would think Bill had made up one but I'd look in the dictionary and there it would be. That's one thing Bill did for all of us. He made us become familiar with our dictionaries."

Conrad Aiken thinks of Faulkner's obsessions with particular words as a "parrotlike mechanical mytacism" or stammer, a compulsion to go on repeating, almost endlessly, such favorites as (Aiken's choices) "myriad, sourceless, impalpable, outrageous, risible, and profound." His impatience with Faulkner's overparenthesized sentences is even greater, but we shall deal with that objection later on. Warren Beck sees more than mere prolixity in Faulkner's tendency to pile up words. He believes that many of these "word-series" may have a definite place in Faulkner's peculiarly analytical style: "In their typical form they are not redundant, however elaborate, and sometimes their cumulative effect is undeniable. . . Quite often, too, these series of words, while seemingly extravagant, are a remarkably compressed rendering, as in the phrase 'passionate tragic emphemeral loves of adolescence'." Beck also believes that despite "some rather clotted prose" Faulkner may have perpetrated in the effort, still he is to be complimented for coming closer than anyone else to "Shakespeare's imperial and opulent use of words" in trying to approximate older literary uses — dramatic chorus, prologue and epilogue, soliloquy, extended speech — all of them demanding, as Volpe has pointed out, an *oral* (even *oratorical*) style in which words pour forth uninhibitedly. "The aim of any such device," Beck says, "is not objective realism but revelation of theme, a revelation raised by the unstinted resourcefulness and power of its language to the highest ranges of imaginative outlook."

FAULKNER AND SOUTHERN DIALECTS. Faulkner was especially skilled in the reproduction of Southern dialects. Because he cared so much for language and its apparently limitless powers; and because he was also sensitively attuned to the syntax, diction, tone and melody *of speech,* he was able to reproduce with remarkable fidelity (and with a minimum of violation of standard spelling) the dialects of his white and Black Mississippi characters. Almost as if he had recorded them on tape or transcribed in some phonetic script (as George Bernard Shaw is said to have done in preparing to write *Pygmalion*), he reproduced the slow drawl of the Southern Negro and the distinctive tone and melody of the redneck's speech pattern, the more refined diction of the educated townspeople and the assumed pomposities of tone and diction of the phonies. All his characters (even those New Englanders who appear in *The Sound and The Fury* in the Quentin section, for example) speak in their own language, and so do the narrators, when he uses them.

NARRATIVE STRUCTURE AND TECHNIQUE. Volpe attributes much of Faulkner's greatness to what he calls the author's "stereoscopic vision" or rare ability "to deal with the specific and the universal simultaneously, to make the real symbolic without sacrificing reality." One can add to this skill another of Faulkner's great attributes, "stereophonic hearing," or rare ability to hear the specific tones of the spoken language and the more subtle undertones and overtones of the language. Granted that Volpe is not speaking of Faulkner's *literal* vision as we may be speaking of his literal hearing; the fact remains that Faulkner (like James Joyce, for example) was more of an *aural* than a *visual* writer, and so we may be permitted to speak of the author's stereoscopic *and* stereophonic vision (the word in its broader sense, of course) as his incomparable skill.

To achieve those added dimensions in his narratives, Faulkner frequently abandoned the "linear" approach, that is, putting together a well-made piece of imaginative writing in which there is a neat, identifiable pattern of events proceeding from a precise beginning to a precise end. Instead, he chose to break up and mix up his time sequences; to fragment his narrative and assign the fragments to a variety of narrators, participants, and observers (in *As I Lay Dying*, there are fifteen such "participants" and sixty fragments); and to load his prose with lyric intensities and other distractions, so that, as Howe points out, "the very effort to read a Faulkner novel forces one into an act of aesthetic and moral discovery, parallel to those discoveries his narrators make in the course of telling their stories." (Which, in essence, is the whole point of Faulkner's narrative style — to involve the reader in the story almost as much as the narrator or character is involved.)

**FAULKNER AS SHORT-STORY WRITER.** One of the difficulties that arise in following a Faulkner narrative is the reader's inability (or refusal) to accept Faulkner's definition of a novel. There are many critics who see some of his novels (for example, *The Unvanquished* and *Go Down, Moses*) as merely collections of short stories. Cowley, in a letter to Faulkner, wrote, "You know my theory, expressed somewhere in the essay — that you are at your best on two levels, either in long stories that can be written in one burst of energy, like *The Bear* and *Spotted Horses* and *Old Man*, or (and) in the Yoknapatawpha cycle as a whole." And in a letter to Marshall Best, Cowley more specifically said that Faulkner's "novels are most of them composed of stories, which is their greatest structural fault." And he adds, in other places, that many of these stories can stand alone, independent of their "host novels," and could thus be published most conveniently in *The Portable Faulkner* (which he was editing at the time). Volpe concurs with Cowley that the majority of Faulkner's novels are "either thematic expansions of narratives little longer than short stories or they are fusions of short stories." We shall see in the next chapter of this book how *The Sound and The Fury* actually began as a short story, and as far as narrative action or structure is concerned, *is* little more than a short story. In structuring his novels (with the rare exceptions of *Intruder in the Dust* and *The Reivers*), Faulkner often achieved a thematic (and sometimes, but not very often) and structural unity by joining in a form of forced literary marriage stories which were concerned with the same family or clan.

FRAGMENTING CHRONOLOGICAL TIME. Slightly disparate narratives (or short stories) having been joined together, the reader is now content to provide any necessary bridges between these narratives. But that would be too simple; Faulkner now proceeds to juxtapose stories (or fragments of stories) of the past with stories (or fragments of stories) of the present. Jean-Paul Sartre attributes the extensive use of this device to Faulkner's preoccupation with the past, a preoccupation that is "so strong that he sometimes disguises the present — and the present makes its way in the shadows, like an underground river, to reappear only when it has become past." (We shall have more to say about Sartre's essay on Faulkner's fragmenting of chronological time later on.) No act, no thought, is isolated in time. "By deliberately breaking up the chronology of his narrative," Volpe says, "Faulkner also dramatizes his recognition that though the human body must exist in chronological time, the mind does not function within the barriers imposed on the body. The mind fuses past, present, and future." And so does Faulkner, in particular, and most admirably, in *The Sound and The Fury*. Through this type of "montage structuring," Volpe concedes that Faulkner was able to combine twentieth-century realistic techniques with the techniques of two of his favorite nineteenth-century authors, the metaphysical novelists, Melville and Hawthorne.

THIRD-PERSON NARRATOR. In the early novels, such as *Sartoris, Sanctuary,* and *Light in August,* Faulkner was content to use the objective, impersonal third-person narrator, mainly because it provided the author with a great deal of freedom in the development of his story and in the handling of his characters. The author may now be omniscient and shuttle back and forth between characters, telling the reader just what is going on in the mind and heart of each of them. Henry James was, of course, the master exploiter of author omniscience; Faulkner adopted this technique because it afforded him the chance to probe deeply and realistically into the ways of the human mind, and made some interesting changes in the technique, especially in *Light in August* and *Intruder in the Dust,* changes we shall discuss in the section on *Themes.*

INTERIOR MONOLOGUE. In *The Sound and The Fury* and *As I Lay Dying,* Faulkner preferred to use the method of subjective revelation of character through "free association," stream of consciousness, inner voices and reflections, long and short drafts, as it were, on the character's "memory fund." The first three sections of *The Sound and The Fury* are Faulkner's own adaptations of the interior monologue technique (the fourth and final section is third-person narration). *As I Lay Dying* displayed still another Faulkner variation on the interior monologue — the narrative carried exclusively through the monologues of fifteen characters. Despite the success he had with this technique in both these early novels, Faulkner still felt it would be better for him to tell his stories through narrators (as would any "straight" or conventional storyteller). In short, if the narrator was good enough for Dickens, Balzac, and Henry James, it would have to be good enough for him.

STORY-WITHIN-A-STORY NARRATION. Faulkner, however, not being a conventional storyteller, made his own (or did he borrow it from Proust?) changes in narrative technique. For example, in the case of the story-within-a-story narrative technique, the narrator can frequently and freely make the association between a current or present event which he is experiencing with the remembrance of an event past, thereby expanding the significance of the main narrative by showing how events earlier in his life or before his life began are all parts of his total personality, his total mind, and (biologically) his total body. Faulkner is saying, in effect, "We are what we were."

MULTIPLE NARRATORS. Japanese literature (and also Japanese films; for example, *Rashomon*) is fond of the technique whereby one story is told by two or more narrators or characters, thereby giving the reader more than one point of view of the same event or series of events. Faulkner used a similar narrative technique in *Absalom, Absalom!*, for example, wherein four narrators tell the same story, or constituent parts of the same story. None of the four narrators can (or should) be identified with the author's point of view. None of them is his "mouthpiece." This is Faulkner's way of presenting an objective view of reality. The end results of this method are (1) to explore the nature of reality, or ontology, or how the mind "processes" the information concerning external events perceived through the senses; and (2) to bring the reader into the characters' (and author's) search for meaning and truth, thus adding still another dimension to the meaning of the story itself.

NARRATIVE AND THEMATIC SYMBOLS. A *narrative* symbol is defined as a symbol used to develop an individual scene or story within a novel. Honeysuckle (in itself a symbol of sexual desire) is used in the second section of *The Sound and The Fury* to represent the complex relationship between Quentin and Caddy, that is, the repressed incestuous feelings of both of them. A *thematic* symbol serves to develop and expand the theme of the whole novel rather than that of the isolated narrative unit in which it occurs. Again, in *The Sound and The Fury* the image of the idiot, Benjy, holding a broken-stemmed narcissus in the surrey, serves as a thematic symbol. In one interpretation, Benjy symbolizes modern man, "inarticulate in a man-centered world without love or moral values."

MYTHOLOGICAL AND BIBLICAL ALLUSIONS. It would be expected of a Southern writer brought up in a Fundamentalist milieu that he would use his familiarity with the Bible. In *Requiem for a Nun*, Gowan Stevens may be said to be playing Adam to Temple Drake's Eve. In *Light in August* and in *The Sound and The Fury* (and obviously in the very title of *Absalom, Absalom!*) the Biblical parallels are many. As we shall explain in detail later, the present action in *The Sound and The Fury* takes place during Easter Friday, Saturday, and Sunday (Quentin's last day, June 2, 1910, is a Thursday, and presumed to be "Holy Thursday" or "Maundy Thursday," preceding Good Friday). And Benjy is thirty-three years old, as was Jesus when He was crucified.

Then there are mythological allusions, not unexpected in a man who spent many of his younger years reading Keats and other Romantic poets. As Faulkner switches from the more Bible-centered Sartorises, Compsons, and De Spains to the more materialistic and earthy Snopeses, mythological allusions become more prominent. The pursuit of Eula Varner by the local studs in *The Hamlet* is compared to Helen and the Trojan War. If Temple Drake is compared to Eve, then more versatile Eula is not only Helen and Eve, but also Semiramis and Lilith. The progression from Caddy to Temple Drake to Eula Varner is marked with allusions to woman as temptress and earth goddess (all three, ironically, desired by inhibited or impotent men — Quentin, Popeye, and Flem Snopes).

TIME AND NARRATIVE FLOW. As indicated earlier, there is no doubt that Faulkner's idiosyncratic concept of time had much to do with the way he modified narrative techniques. Faulkner's characters, says Sartre, are helpless because they are committed to the past. The point of view of a Faulkner character is described by Sartre as that of a passenger looking backward from a speeding car. What he sees is the landscape over which he is traveling flowing *away* from him. There is no future in view, the present is one large blur; only the past is clearly visible as it streams away before his backward-looking gaze. Cleanth Brooks interprets Sartre's metaphor as follows: "Man's very freedom is bound up with his sense of having some kind of future. Unless he can look ahead to the future, he is not free."

SYMBOLISM. When asked by a University of Virginia student if the title in the novel, *Pylon*, was symbolic, if it referred to the girl as a marker or beacon around which all the men gravitated, Faulkner answered: "Now there's some more of this erudite professorial symbolism gets into everything. I'm sure that you're quite right. I just hadn't thought of that. I'm glad to know it. I'll remember that and I'll use that some time probably." Later, another student asked him if there was a symbol (a thematic symbol?) in *The Bear*. This time Faulkner was much less naive and explained that the bear represents the vanishing wilderness, the little dog that the bear couldn't scare symbolizes the indomitable spirit of man, and that he would go back and dig up some more symbols "because I have learned around an even dozen that I put into that story *without knowing it . . .*" (Italics added) John Faulkner felt that too many people try to read too much into his brother's writings; however, *it is just a little too hard to swallow the idea that Faulkner was a naive writer who rarely, if ever, used symbols consciously.* Storytelling and symbolism are not necessarily incompatible; the first storytellers, the myth-makers, were pretty good performers, and no one will deny the highly symbolic value of most myths. *Simply and bluntly, in our opinion, Faulkner consciously and skillfully employed symbolism.* It is also hard to ignore a statement Faulkner made, also in answer to a University of Virginia student's question: "I wanted to be a poet, and I think of myself now as a failed poet, not as a novelist at all but a failed poet who had to take up what he could do." Poets, according to most literary authorities, favor symbolic language, and poets, even would-be poets and failed poets who read much of Symbolist poetry, favor symbolic language beyond the normal extent.

SYMBOL, ALLEGORY, AND MYTH. When it was suggested that Faulkner might have consciously and deliberately intended *Absalom, Absolom!* as a connected and logical allegory, Cowley attempted to analyze the process whereby Faulkner came up with symbols in his stories, whether he willed it or not. First, Faulkner was writing a story; the story affected him deeply; he brooded over it. Then, in a more or less unconscious manner, "the incidents in the story came to represent the forces and elements in the social situation, since the mind naturally works in terms of symbols and parallels." This form of symbolism, or what Cowley chooses to call "parallelism," pervades the whole fictional framework (mainly Yoknapatawpha) that Faulkner was elaborating in novel after novel, until, Cowley concludes, "his work has become a myth or legend of the South."

Cleanth Brooks was also not satisfied with Faulkner's ingenuous disclaimers concerning the use of symbols. He could detect a complete allegorical pattern for *Sanctuary,* for example, in which Temple Drake is the South, raped by modern industry (symbolized by Popeye), except that modern industry and the civilization it has spawned, being sterile and impotent, had to get a substitute to rape her. *Pylon* likewise includes a scene in the airplane involving a sterile reporter, and there, too, the symbolism is obvious to everybody except Faulkner.

Cowley, Brooks and others have been able to ascertain a definite symbolic outline in Faulkner's fiction. There are many symbolic motifs in Faulkner's writings, and Robert Penn Warren suggests a few for further study: images of the hunt, the flight, the pursuit; the important symbolic relationship between man and earth (see below under *Themes* for a more comprehensive treatment of this relationship);

the contrast between images of compulsion and images of will or freedom; and the "frozen moment," the arrested action (most notably favored today in current motion pictures in the form of stop-action) which in itself becomes symbolic.

Finally, Howe calls our attention to the multiplicity of symbols, references, and echoes derived from Christian theology, tradition, and custom. There are embodiments of simple Christian virtue, especially in the form of Dilsey in *The Sound and The Fury*, but also Byron Bunch, Isaac McCaslin, and others. There are also several figures and emblems of the Crucifixion, the story of Jesus, and other reflections of stern Fundamentalist teachings and doctrines under which Faulkner was brought up. These symbols are far from accidental, as we shall attempt to show in the section on *Themes*.

MAJOR THEMES IN FAULKNER. Someone once summarized all of human existence as a struggle or conflict between man and man, man and nature, and man and himself. Someone else was quick to pounce upon this observation and to convert it to what he then referred to as the three major themes of literature: man against man, man against nature, and man against himself. Faulkner, among many other writers, subscribed to this conclusion, and then proceeded to provide these basic themes with his own distinctive dimensions and coloration. In his works, then, the major themes may be described as follows:

MODERN SOCIETY AS A WASTELAND. Without being indebted to T. S. Eliot for anything else but the metaphor itself, Faulkner saw in the impersonal, mechanized, industrialized society a force that was dehumanizing man (both in the South and elsewhere) by persuading him to give up the traditional, essential values — courage, fortitude, honor, pride, and goodness — for the deceptively attractive false values based on the love of money.

INDIVIDUAL AS PRISONER OF THE PAST. Perhaps because he himself often felt bound to the past, Faulkner perceived all his heroes as prisoners of the past, of society, of social taboos and moral inhibitions, and of their own introspectiveness and consciousness. The Faulknerian hero looks back longingly to the 19th-century pioneer, that rugged individualist who was absolutely free to control his destiny to the extent that any human being could in a universe governed by chance; or, as one critic has described Faulkner's view of human life, "cosmic pessimism" based on a peculiar combination of Fundamentalist predestination and scientific determinism.

SOCIALIZATION LEADS TO LOSS OF FREEDOM. To Faulkner, social man, or the individual as the end-product of a process of psychological conditioning, has been deprived of all chance of responding naturally and positively to the experiences and influences of his existence. A "heritage of codes and concepts" established by his parents, his relatives, and his society determines his very feelings, thoughts, and actions. As a result, throughout his life the individual (that is, the social man) must contend with the past, and must accept the fact that his responses to immediate and real experiences will be conditioned by that past, so that he will be incapable of a "feeling response to life."

WILDERNESS AS OUR LOST EDEN. Social man was once primitive, natural man. Before society began to encroach upon the wilderness, the natural man existed in every human being. But now, this confused and fragmented social man, all that is natural smothered within him, is alienated from his own consciousness and from the world of nature. The fundamental conflict that arises from this condition is that between social man's attempt at a logical and rational view of existence and primitive man's unquestioning acceptance of all life.

Social man can find no satisfying answers to his cosmic

questions about life and death, and is therefore disabled by increasing disillusionment and finally falls into black despair. Primitive, natural man, on the other hand, finds no need to explain or interpret life or death. Through his unquestioning acceptance of these two basic phenomena in nature, he is able to achieve an enviable peace of mind and real strength to cope with the struggle for existence.

SOUTH'S GUILT IS EVERY WHITE MAN'S GUILT. Almost without exception, Faulkner's heroes are deeply burdened with the guilt which their ancestors incurred when they first enslaved the Negro people. The white boy taught to keep the Negro in his place is as much a victim of the Jim Crow restrictions as the Negro because such a response to another human being is not natural. If that same white boy should be honest enough to admit that the Negro is not his inferior, his "natural" servant, he would be defying that heritage of codes and concepts mentioned earlier, and would thus be alienating himself from his family, his society, and his heritage.

PURITANISM AND FUNDAMENTALISM DENY NATURE. Modern man has become separated from his God by the abstractions of theology and narrowly drawn religious customs and practices. Consequently, he is involved with shadows and symbols of reality rather than with reality itself. As for Faulkner's characters (and very probably Faulkner himself), they are also bound by Calvinistic Puritanism which frequently prevents them from observing love, sex and women in a natural, wholesome manner. Faulkner himself manifests this inhibition by making many of his women promiscuous or prostitutes (Caddy, Temple Drake, Eula Varner, *et al*), and many of his men impotent (Flem Snopes), perverts (Popeye), castrates (Benjy), or sexually inhibited romantics (Quentin Compson). As Edith Hamilton has observed, "Young women are not really human to him. He calls them 'the Symbol of the ancient and eternal Snake.' . . . The relation between the sexes, indeed, always becomes a crucial difficulty. . . . All that had to do with the flesh was tainted and all that had to do with sex was the most fleshly and the most tainted of all. . . . He is to the very depths of him a Puritan, a violently twisted Puritan, a perverted Puritan, and that means something very strange indeed. . . ."

Hamilton's opinion is shared by several other critics, particularly Leslie Fiedler (we shall deal with his critique later) and Robert Penn Warren. The latter observes that Faulkner's admirable women are those "conspicuously beyond the age of sexual distraction." Their role is to run a household and offer the fruits of intuitive wisdom. They are "beyond the magical powers of sexuality." But the younger women (with the possible exception of Linda Snopes in *The Mansion*) are never free from Faulkner's bitter attitude toward them. So persistent is this dis-ease with the doings of "woman-flesh," says Warren, "that it cannot be dismissed as a vagary of either Faulkner or the characters who convey it."

The last word on this last of the major themes is provided by Rabi, who notes that Faulkner often associates the sexual act with vomiting, a sense or feeling of disgust that illustrates even further the nature of Faulkner's fundamental clash with the living, contemporary world. It is the same disgust, displeasure, and despair that seemingly runs through five of the six themes discussed. "What meanings can acts have," asks Rabi, "when they are only empty manifestations, deprived of any real link with concrete reality?" It may be an unreal world, but it is the only world, apparently, as seen best through the eyes of Quentin Compson (and Faulkner?). It is also an unreal world of Mrs. Compson (in *The Sound and the Fury*) who puts on black mourning veils, cries, and declares between sobs that Caddy is dead because Caddy (at that time a mere fifteen years at most, but by Faulkner's standards mature in the ways of sex) was caught kissing a boy. "If words are always lies," Rabi concludes, "acts must often seem ambiguous," or at the least unreal. This, then, is Faulkner's world, a world in which life is a walking shadow, a tale told by an idiot, full of sound and fury, signifying — nothing. And Faulkner is, perhaps, the consummate "cosmic pessimist" of the twentieth century.

EARLIER NOVELS: 1926-1940. From the very beginning of his career as a novelist, Faulkner attempted to provide a critique of modern life both in the South and in those areas not exclusively related to Southern society. In providing such a critique, he joined other American writers in examining the many dominant and recurrent themes of twentieth-century literature — the decline of moral values under the onslaught of a growing commercialism and industrialization, the increasing incapacity for establishing close human relationships, the encroachment of an impersonal world and its terrifying by-product, alienation, and the loss of sensitivity before the growing acceptance of a vulgarity and rapacity that those in power insisted had to be equated with modern progress and America's growth as a world power. In nine of the twelve novels that he wrote during this first period (1926-1940), Yoknapatawpha County provided the society in microcosm upon which Faulkner based his critique. (In the list that follows below, the *non*-Yoknapatawpha novels will be indicated by an asterisk.)

*SOLDIER'S PAY* (1926). Faulkner wrote his first novel, *Soldier's Pay*, while living among the Bohemians who crowded around Sherwood Anderson in New Orleans. Faulkner said that he began the novel with the principle that novels should deal with imaginary scenes and people; so the portraits of spiritually maimed veterans of World War I, virtually living corpses, were not based on his own direct experience, and the novel itself was laid in Georgia, where he had never been. The novel was written to accommodate what Faulkner judged to be popular taste, and was conceived in the then fashionable *fin de siècle* tradition. While he was abroad in July 1925, Faulkner received a $200 advance on the book from publisher Horace Liveright (on the strong recommendation of Sherwood Anderson). The money helped to keep Faulkner in Europe for awhile longer, and by the time he came home the novel was published, and "bombed." Liveright began to have his doubts about Faulkner as a novelist.

*MOSQUITOES* (1927). After *Mosquitoes* was published, and also "bombed," Liveright canceled the three-year contract to which he had signed Faulkner. His second novel was also written under influence of the supersophisticated, world-weary, New Orleans Bohemian crowd. Faulkner intended it to be a novel in the manner of Aldous Huxley's *Point Counterpoint*. Cowley called it a very bad novel, and Faulkner concurred.

*SARTORIS* (1929). In *Sartoris,* Faulkner turned for the first time to what he really knew, to subjective and local materials, to that piece of land of which he was "sole owner and proprietor" — Yoknapatawpha County. The book has been described by Malcolm Cowley as "a romantic and partly unconvincing novel, but with many fine scenes in it. . . ." The hero, young Bayard Sartoris, has been identified by many critics (and even by Faulkner himself) as to some extent a projection of Faulkner's romanticized image of himself; and both the Old Colonel and the Young Colonel (based to a large extent on earlier — and more daring — members of the Faulkner clan) make their first appearance in Faulkner fiction. The book is also important because it stated most of the themes the author would later expand in the Yoknapatawpha series. The novel's main theme is the juxtaposition of the present with the past, with the author rooting for the past. As far as the real, authentic Faulkner is concerned, *Sartoris* was his first novel.

*THE SOUND AND THE FURY* (1929). Since this novel is the main subject of this study, we shall discuss it in detail in subsequent chapters.

*AS I LAY DYING* (1930). Faulkner said it took him "just about six weeks in the spare time from a twelve-hour-a-day job at manual labor" to write *As I Lay Dying,* his fifth novel. It was easy to write because all the material was already at hand. This was a Yoknapatawpha family, and Faulkner, from what he knew of such families, seemed to be saying that even the Bundrens could come together for a brief act of humanity, when properly motivated by the incipient death of someone dearly beloved, in a way the once proud and aristocratic Compsons *(As I Lay Dying* is at once a contrast and a companion-piece to *The Sound and The Fury)* no longer could. The novel is also the shortest of all of Faulkner's novels, but for a novel that was written on the bottom of a wheelbarrow (Faulkner claimed), it is a very finished one indeed.

*SANCTUARY* (1931). Faulkner really surfaced as an established American novelist with *Sanctuary.* It was the first of his books to really sell. "He told me," John Faulkner writes, "that he couldn't get people to read his other books so he decided to write one they would. He sat down one day to think of what would be the most horrible thing he could put in a book and came up with idea of a man using a corncob on a girl." Faulkner himself said it was "a cheap idea, deliberately conceived to make money." Perhaps that is really how the book came to be; but it is hard to tell sometimes if Faulkner is being serious or ironic, or merely trying to pass off a "tall tale" about himself in his characteristically mock-humble manner. The statement about the book's having been written for money was made in the author's own preface to the Modern Library edition of 1932. And, since few critics will believe that a book is good because its author says it is, they will, on the other hand, hesitate to believe that a book is bad because its author says it is. As part of that same preface, Faulkner had also said that "I tore the galleys down and rewrote the book. It had already been set up once, so I had to pay for the privilege of rewriting it, trying to make out of it something which would not shame *The Sound and The Fury* and *As I Lay Dying* too much and I made a fair job. . . ."

*Sanctuary* was an immediate popular success. It sold even in Oxford. But people there usually asked to have it wrapped in plain brown paper. The whole town was shocked and scandalized to think that a Southern gentleman could write such a book. Cowley says that Faulkner was not trying to shock the bourgeoisie so much as to startle and affront them, "quite literally, knock them off their pins." Leslie Fiedler sees in *Sanctuary* "on the one hand, the darkest of all Faulkner's books, a brutal protest to the quality of American life written in the pit of the Great Depression; but on the other hand, it is the dirtiest of all the dirty jokes exchanged among men only at the expense of the abdicating Anglo-Saxon Virgin."

Faulkner's father apparently agreed with Fiedler. Even though the book made Faulkner a great deal of money, initiated an invitation to come to Hollywood, and brought the recognition that he had long waited for from the critical community, his father was greatly distressed by the book. In fact, if we are to believe John Faulkner, he even tried to have the book suppressed and withdrawn from the bookstores.

One of Faulkner's more conscientious supporters has suggested that there was more than venality and greed in Faulkner's decision to write *Sanctuary*. Whatever the reasons for writing that preface, Faulkner did not invent a highly charged sex story just to startle the public. "In dealing with the startling real events," Carvell Collins says, "Faulkner by no means exaggerated them for cheap effect — quite to the contrary, he reduced their horror, besides doing the more important work of giving them form of a high order." Collins goes on to relate how Faulkner acquired the raw (unprocessed, that is, not the connotative meaning of "improper") material for the novel while with a woman companion in a night club during the mid-1920's. "A girl who at present may be identified as N. came across the room," Collins writes, "sat down at their table, and in half an hour told them an interesting part of her autobiography. A few years later it became the core of *Sanctuary*. . . ." Faulkner thought about that "autobiography" for some years and tried to write that story in several ways, drawing upon related events in that same girl's life which he knew of from other reliable sources.

Whatever else Collins may be trying to prove (that, for example, Faulkner was not a mere sensationalist or low-key, Southern pornographer), Faulkner cannot be accused of having had a dirty mind. Nor is *Sanctuary* a mere dirty book or a "mere accumulation of pointless horrors." It may very well be what Cleanth Brooks has called it — an allegory of the rape and corruption of the South by modern industrialization and commercialism. As such, it plays an important part in almost all of Faulkner's novels in the Yoknapatawpha series, and must therefore be considered a milestone and a turning-point in Faulkner's development as a writer. It is also, from the technical point of view, one of Faulkner's most skillfully written novels in that it is (according to Cowley) "an example of the Freudian method turned backward, being full of sexual nightmares that are in reality social symbols."

*LIGHT IN AUGUST* (1932). The theme of this book is lostness and loneliness, or the human condition in the Yoknapatawpha of the 1930's as shaped by hatred and martyrdom, isolation and alienation, and social divisiveness. The novel is basically a trilogy (or triad) of three stories — of Lena Grove, Joe Christmas, and the Reverend Hightower. Lena Grove, pregnant and serene, bears up stoically throughout the conflict and confusion of the book as if she were the symbol of the very basic principle of human survival. Joe Christmas, a Christological figure if ever there was one *(despite Faulkner's usual disclaimers about conscious symbolism)*, is a white man who believes that he has mixed blood in him, and so cannot easily identify himself with the white *or* the Negro community. He may be the South, confused by the doubts about his own identity. Joe finally winds up a martyr to both the intolerance and vindictiveness of society and his own heroic striving toward some semblance of human dignity. The Reverend Hightower is a man of good will, but of no help to Joe or anybody else involved in the conflicts of the modern South because he has been made impotent by delusional memories of the past. The contrast between the fate of Lena Grove and that of Joe Christmas poses a discrepancy that Faulkner believed reflected the very outrage of existence.

*PYLON* (1935). John Faulkner tells us that his brother was mad about flying, and even when he came out of the service he continued to tinker with planes and fly them whenever he got the chance. During Faulkner's stay in New Orleans, the Gates Flying Circus came to town, and Faulkner happily accepted the invitation of this barnstorming outfit to do some wing-walking with them. The Circus turned up later in *Pylon*, which is all about a family of stunt flyers.

*ABSALOM, ABSALOM!* (1936). Of this novel, Malcolm Cowley has said that "though at first it strikes us as being pitched in too high a key, [it] is structurally the soundest of all the novels in the Yoknapatawpha series — and it gains power in retrospect." Cowley also believed that it belonged in the category of Gothic romances, what with its frequent abandonment of the principal theme of Colonel Sutpen's design for his manorial Sutpen's Hundred for the secondary theme of incest and miscegenation. The style of the novel is ambivalent, sometimes grand, sometimes almost hysterical. Thomas Sutpen, amoral, willful plantation owner living in the 1850's, may serve as a symbol of the entire Southern experience. "With a little cleverness," Cowley has observed, "the whole novel might be explained as a connected and logical allegory . . ." But then, the same thing has been said about *Sanctuary* and even about *The Sound and The Fury*. Faulkner's answer was always the same: he was trying to write a story that would be so powerful that it would involve the reader almost as strongly as it had involved the author.

*THE UNVANQUISHED* (1938). *The Unvanquished* was published originally as a collection of five short stories from the time of the Civil War, with young Bayard (later to become Colonel) Sartoris as their major figure. The collection was then revised for a novel form. The revision or transformation evolved, even though at first Faulkner didn't think of the collection in terms of a novel: they were too episodic to serve as coherent elements of a novel. Then Faulkner thought of them as a series of stories, with Bayard and his Negro friend, Ringo, providing the interrelating agents. "When I got into the first one," Faulkner explained, "I could see two more, but by the time I'd finished the first one I saw that it was going further than that, and then when I'd finished the fourth one, I had postulated too many questions that I had to answer for my own satisfaction. So the others had to be — the other three or two, whichever it was, had to be written then." Since Faulkner had employed a similar technique in his other novels, it is fair and proper to accept *The Unvanquished* as a novel.

*THE WILD PALMS* (1939). Here again we have the problem of a bifurcated novel — the "Wild Palms" story and the "Old Man" story. *The Wild Palms* is a novel with two plots alternating throughout the chapters as it tells the story of two people, Harry and Charlotte, "who sacrificed everything for love, and then lost that." As good as the "Wild Palms" story may be, it needs the "Old Man" story to give it the pitch and intensity to sustain it as a piece of fiction. "Old Man" (as in "Old Man River") takes the reader out of Yoknapatawpha, but not out of Mississippi. It is the story of a man "who got his love and spent the rest of the book fleeing from it, even to the extent of voluntarily going back to jail where he would be safe" (Faulkner's description).

*THE HAMLET* (1940). *The Hamlet*, the Snopeses' first "starring vehicle," is a "racy comic extravaganza which borrows from the American tradition of the tall tale" (Howe), and a kind of "prose fantasia" (Warren Beck) in which the author's multiform style created various episodes about the Snopeses, that "verminlike clan which spreads its corruption and nihilism over the entire surface of Yoknapatawpha" (Howe).

The episodes make use of (in addition to the colloquial tall tales or whoppers) "poetic description, folk humor, deliberative reflective narration, swift cryptic drama, and even a grotesque allegory, of Snopes in hell" (Beck). The book introduces a newer Faulkner, more relaxed, heartier in tone, and less of the Southerner preoccupied with the collective guilt of his threatened world. As in many of his earlier books, Faulkner said that *The Hamlet* was "incepted as a novel." The "inception" produced only "Spotted Horses." Two years later, Faulkner's main character, Ratliff the sewing-machine agent, "inspired" him to write "The Hound," "Jamshyd's Courtyard," and then, with the "arrival' of the Snopes clan, "Mule in the Yard," "Brass," "Barn Burning," and "Wash," the four latter stories eventually spotted in other novels. With *The Hamlet* launched, the reader now had a long wait for the other two novels in the trilogy, *The Town* (1957) and *The Mansion* (1959).

LATER NOVELS. The relaxed style of Faulkner's later novels, the free-wheeling approach that relied so heavily on high jinks in plot construction and high-powered rhetoric all too reminiscent of dead Southern oratory, may very well have indicated a serious decline in creative energy. From 1940 on (with some memorable exceptions), fiction (for Faulkner) would be synonymous with escape.

*GO DOWN, MOSES* (1942). Like many of Faulkner's other novels, this is a collection of stories interwoven and interrelated by the use of identical themes. The main theme is the relationship between whites and Negroes. That would be the *social* theme. The *philosophical* theme, as exemplified most vividly in "The Bear," the centerpiece of the total book, is the need for man to recapture and reassert an attitude of respect and reverence for the land around him. In Isaac McCaslin, the main character (and probably a projection of Faulkner himself), we have the first of the *transcendental* ecologists. Through the teaching and example of Sam Fathers, the Negro-Indian "man of the wilderness," Isaac finally rejects that Southern heritage based on defilement of the wilderness and the land to live as a poor and innocent carpenter. The religious parallel implied in this decision — Jesus was a carpenter, the meek shall inherit the earth, etc. — is not too subtle.

*INTRUDER IN THE DUST* (1948). As with *Sanctuary,* Faulkner was not aiming for Hollywood when he wrote *Intruder in the Dust.* Nonetheless, it was made into a fairly successful film in 1949, and even had its premiere in Oxford, Mississippi. Faulkner intended it as another novel on race relations, with a Negro as hero (a not unusual choice for Faulkner). The novel started with the idea of a black man in jail for a crime he did not commit, but destined to be executed nevertheless on the basis of "circumstantial evidence" and the prevailing suspicion of and bias toward Blacks. Lucas Beauchamp, the black man, couldn't hire a detective, "couldn't hire one of these tough guys that slapped women around, took a drink every time he couldn't think of what to say next." (Note how Faulkner's description of the typical Hollywood detective reveals the kinds of stories he had been working on in Hollywood — "The Big Sleep" by Raymond Chandler, for example, with Philip Marlowe, man-about-town detective.) The novel was intended as a detective story, but once Faulkner began to concentrate more fully on Lucas, then Lucas "took charge of the story and the story was a good deal different from the idea that — of the detective story that I had started with." It was still a better-than-average *whodunit,* a fact which Hollywood never lost track of.

*REQUIEM FOR A NUN* (1951). There are several theories about this novel in the form of a three-act drama, with narrative prologues to each act, about the later life of Temple Drake. One, that Faulkner, like Henry James, whom he read, respected, emulated, and was often compared with, was a frustrated dramatist. Two, that Faulkner, having been re-recognized by the American public through *Intruder in the Dust* (both the novel and the film), wished to capitalize on the earlier popularity of *Sanctuary,* and so brought back Temple Drake (this time supported by the "nun," Nancy, the self-sacrificing black woman). Three, that Faulkner was a master writer of dialogue — probably the main reason why he was called out to Hollywood so often — and naturally wanted to exploit that talent to the fullest through the dramatic form. The latter explanation seems to us, at least, the most reasonable. In any event, Paris and Greece saw fit to give the novel-play a stage production.

*A FABLE* (1954). There had been much critical talk about the decline in the quality of Faulkner's writing after 1940. With *A Fable,* published four years after Faulkner's receiving of the Nobel Prize, the critics appeared to have been vindicated. The novel was a colossal flop, its sanctimoniousness probably influenced by the dignity and sobriety newly acquired with the Nobel Prize. It was intended to be a pacifist tract, with a simple French corporal assuming the Christ role to lead twelve soldier-apostles in a peace strike in the midst of a battle in World War I. The symbolism is heavy and unconvincing, the religiosity unappealing, and the book is shot through with long, obscure, highly rhetorical soliloquies that come between the reader and his efforts to comprehend what is going on. Nothing is said or revealed directly if it can be done by reflection (as if with mirrors, perhaps). The book is tedious, overblown, and, as one critic put it, "seems demented."

*THE TOWN* (1957). Faulkner seemed to be back on safer, more familiar ground with this book, the second in the Snopes trilogy. *The Hamlet* told the story of what happened to the Southern crossroads community of Frenchman's Bend, around the turn of the century, when it was invaded by the rapacious, vermin-like Snopeses. *The Town* chronicles the history of Snopesism in Jefferson from Flem Snopes' arrival there as part owner of a little restaurant around 1908, until he becomes bank president (with the help of his flirtatious wife Eula) in 1927. The events are narrated, a chapter at a time, by three of Faulkner's most important "characters" or "stock-company players": V. K. Ratcliff, Gavin Stevens, and Chick Mallison. By using the different points of view of the three narrators, the formal structure of the novel is given unusual variety and vitality. In spite of its serious theme, *The Town* is basically a funny book. In Ratcliff, Faulkner has given the reader a countryman's sense of the comic that is representative of the long tradition of Southern frontier humor that is displayed to its best advantage in Faulkner's last book, *The Reivers.*

*THE MANSION* (1959). The Snopes trilogy concludes with *The Mansion,* a novel that is exceptional because it offers the reader a Snopes *as hero* — Mink Snopes, Flem Snopes' cousin, who has spent thirty-eight years in prison for murder. As Faulkner saw it, prison does rehabilitate, and so a former villain is now a hero. The novel is also memorable for the convincing way in which Faulkner incorporates the Snopeses into universal mankind, and assigns to them the same fate that had been given to the Sartorises, the Compsons, and all the other Southerners "to the mansion born." The Snopeses share the same predicament as the rest of us do — Northerners, Southerners, whites, Blacks, aristocrats, "white trash" — and so one must show Christian mercy and compassion for everybody, including murderers, thieves, prostitutes, and even sewing-machine agents. Yoknapatawpha County is, after all, the South in microcosm; and the South, after all, may very well be considered the whole U.S. in microcosm.

*THE REIVERS* (1962). Faulkner ended his writing career, not with a bang, not with a whimper, but with a laugh, a long, hearty laugh. *The Reivers* is essentially the story of a boy's initiation into manhood, but this time not through the transcendental rituals of the wilderness as in *The Bear*. This time the less-than-pristine pure wilderness is a brothel, and the medium is an ultra-modern vehicle, the automobile. Lucius Priest is the innocent, and Ned McCaslin is the not-so-innocent "Sam Fathers" this time. The events take place in 1905. The little, sleepy county seat of Jefferson is awakened into the twentieth century by arrival of one of the earliest of the automobiles. The author, hitherto rather unfavorably disposed to any manifestations of modernization and mechanization, takes a more optimistic view of things this time; his very friendly treatment of Mr. Buffaloe, the town's mechanical genius, for example, is a throwback perhaps to the very youthful William Faulkner tinkering with gadgets and machines he had read about in *American Boy* magazine. And Faulkner, for his part, can well understand what motivated the three *reivers* (robbers or thieves) — Lucius Priest, Boom Hogganbeck, and Ned McCaslin — to steal the automobile (less intellectual motives notwithstanding). *The Reivers* is consistently, innocently comic in spirit.

# TEXTUAL ANALYSIS OF
## THE SOUND AND THE FURY

THEME AND STRUCTURE: OVERVIEW. This novel, a "book of spectacular literary *purity*, entirely without commercial intent and entirely drawn from his own deepest resources," was Faulkner's first successful literary achievement. It was published in 1929 by Harrison Smith after Harcourt Brace had taken a chance on *Sartoris* and sustained both a literary and a financial loss. *The Sound and The Fury*, however, was an immediate *succès d'estime*, almost completely ignored by the general reading public because of its extreme difficulty, but appealing with tremendous force to "the discriminating few," the critics who would be able in time to form the taste of the intelligent many, and especially Faulkner's peers, whose opinion he valued far above that of the reading public.

The novel is about the Compson family, its decline and fall, and about the "death of a world." It is partly narrated by a 33-year-old idiot, Benjy, whose babblings describe his neurotic parents — Jason Compson III, a most effete intellectual, and Caroline Bascomb Compson, a neurasthenic woman who evades reality through constant claims to a gentility long since passed away; his nymphomaniac sister Caddy, and his neurotic brother Quentin, whose incestuous feelings for his sister ultimately drive him to suicide; his other brother, Jason, superbly comic throughout his extreme rascality; Miss Quentin, Caddy's child, who replicates her mother's perverted habits, eventually robs Jason, and elopes with a circus performer; and Dilsey, the noble Negro housekeeper, who valiantly strives to keep the disintegrating family together, fails, but personally "endures."

The first of four sections of the novel is given over to Benjy, whose "chaotic burden of memory," manifesting itself in a free-associational monologue, "holds the family's past in a purity of suspension." The second section, Quentin's, consists of the stream-of-consciousness, impressionistic fragments of a Hamlet-like, neurotic romantic on the seemingly predestined way to suicide. The third section, an interior monologue, is Jason's version of the tragedy of the Compsons, a fate from which he has been able to escape through the amorality of a commercialism that all the other Compsons have refused to accept as the wave of the future. The final section is given over to a third-person narrator, whose function it is to show how Dilsey and the other Negroes will survive the death of the traditional South, even as the smell of death pervades the very atmosphere and climate of decay, intolerance, and rejection of reality around them. The plot line, although rigidly confined to a single family, suggests a complete awareness of troubles and conflicts that affect *all* human beings, for in the moral and spiritual death of the Compsons, and of Yoknapatawpha as well, is an "acting-out of the disorder of our time."

NAMING THE NOVEL. The title, *The Sound and The Fury*, was taken from Shakepeare's *Macbeth*, Act V, Scene V, lines 19-28. "Yes, there must have been a dozen books titled from that speech," Faulkner said. "I think that I had the best one." Very likely; especially the last three lines of the speech: "it is a tale/Told by an idiot, full of sound and fury,/ Signifying nothing." It would be too simple to say that Faulkner got the idea for Benjy the idiot from those lines; but the "tale" is told, not by an idiot alone but by three other "normal" characters. The "tale," it is true, is full of sound (Faulkner was sound-oriented, a point we hope we established earlier), but its significance is hardly inconsequential. Then, earlier in the speech, one comes upon the lines: "Life's but a walking shadow" and "To the last syllable of recorded time," and one is tempted to plunge into the symbolism of shadows in Quentin's section and into the manner in which

Faulkner fragments time in that same section (and to a lesser degree in the Benjy section), and then simplistically conclude that Faulkner must have hit upon these devices through the inspiration provided by that same speech. Not so, Faulkner said; it was a good speech, and from what he knew about Shakespeare's works, he was smart enough to pick the best book title from the speech. The symbologists and the chronographers will get their day in court in due time (see below) ; for the moment, let it suffice that Faulkner merely liked the *sound* of *The Sound and The Fury* as a title.

STRUCTURE OF NOVEL: ANALYSIS. At the very beginning of the novel, the reader is confronted with a *fait accompli*, namely the collapse of the Compson family. Faulkner can therefore dispense with the usual characteristics of the conventional narrative (for example, suspense) and, instead of beginning at the beginning, begin *at the end*. The thrust of the action or story line (whatever that might be in such a novel) will be backward and take the form of a series of recollections, reflections, and remembrances. (At this point, the reader should recall Sartre's metaphor of people on a train looking back on the distance they have traveled.)

To reconstruct the events leading up to that fateful Easter weekend in 1928, Faulkner required a Compson who had managed either to survive or be present at that time. Mr. Compson was dead; so was Quentin. Caddy was gone; so was her daughter. Mrs. Compson was too preoccupied with herself and her present imaginary ailments. Jason had too little respect for family history to be entrusted with its recapitulation. And Dilsey, although she had carefully observed much of those events and was almost a member of the family, was still too detached to tell the tale. The novel, then, had to be "a tale told by an idiot," Benjy. (Do we contradict ourselves? Then we contradict ourselves. The point is too important to be withheld through a foolish consistency.) The final decision was dictated by the nature of Benjy himself; he alone was able to retain the past in its pristine state, unmodified by human thought and conscious experience. Moreover, unlike Quentin or Jason, he had no clearly delineated point of view to skew his memories. He alone could furnish the reader with the untreated, unprocessed data of the past. He was, in fact, "simply the past forsaken."

At the risk of anticipating material we shall offer later, let us proceed one step further and emphasize the important contribution Benjy makes to the structure of the total novel. In the final chapter we are presented with a few new incidents, not even hinted at in earlier sections. These are (in Howe's fine phrase) "merely bitter footnotes to a text of disaster." Almost everything else was adumbrated by Benjy — the pivotal events, the significant attitudes, the very theme of the novel itself. The Benjy section is more than one of four movements or variations on the theme; it is the "hard nucleus" of the novel, the "symbolic token" of the book.

STRUCTURE REVEALS THEME. The theme of *The Sound and The Fury* is implicit in and interwoven with the structure. It is *the relation between the deed and man's apprehension of the deed, between the deed or act or event and the interpretation thereof.* Consequently, Faulkner, having accepted that theme, proceeded to show how four people reacted to and interpreted a common series of events.

The structure is clearly transparent in the arrangement of events of the evening in which Damuddy (the Compson grandmother) dies. The reader immediately perceives the reactions and attitudes of the four children (Caddy of the muddy drawers, Quentin, Jason, and Benjy) to each other and to the mystery of death itself. The structure is thus immediately fixed and established, but the central situation is intentionally left ambiguous in order to involve the reader more actively in reconstruction of the story. He is also required to peal off layer after layer of significance as he proceeds from one section to the other. There is then (or should be) a gradual (even systematic) clarification of events, a falling into place of fragments of scenes and conversations reported earlier in the Benjy section. *It is imperative, therefore, for the reader to master the Benjy section, to plow through all its difficulties and intricacies to establish for himself a frame of reference within which to comprehend the other three sections.*

KEYSTONE OF THE STRUCTURE. Caddy's loss of her virginity to Dalton Ames (anticipated in the symbol of the muddy drawers) is the keystone or focus of the novel's structure. (It is also logically the source of dramatic tension.) The four sections of the novel may be subtly and inextricably connected, but they are at the same time quite distinct and independent as related to the fact of Caddy's fall from chastity and grace. Each of the first three sections presents its own "true" version of the same facts. None of the three versions — Benjy's, Quentin's, and Jason's — is "the truth, the whole truth, and nothing but the truth." No fact or event is a fact or event in isolation — except perhaps in the Platonic sense — but a piece of the truth as seen through the distorting glass of an individual's eye, mind, and consciousness. The reliability of a witness (or even an eyewitness) is a relative quantity.

The sequence of events which follows is therefore not the end-product of Caddy's "fall" — which could be responded to in several different ways depending on the individual's peculiar value system — but by the special significance which each of Caddy's three brothers attaches to it. Benjy sees in it the loss of the only source of tenderness and affection he has ever known. Quentin equates Caddy's "defection" with the end of honor, purity, innocence, and family pride. Jason sees it as the beginning of a long career of promiscuity — "Once a bitch always a bitch, what I say," even to the next generation, Caddy's daughter. In effect, then, the four sections (we add here the fourth one, in which the author as third-person narrator and "outsider" presents Dilsey's version of the events) seem quite discrete, even though they repeat certain events and are concerned with the same pivotal problem, that is, Caddy's loss of virginity.

THEME REVEALS STRUCTURE. Let us restate the theme in order to emphasize this point: It is the relation between the deed and man's apprehension of the deed, between the deed or act or event and the interpretation thereof. The first three sections, therefore, present *seriatim* a clearly defined and fairly isolated world built around three different versions of the truth. "The fact that Benjy is dumb," Olga Vickery observes, "is symbolic of the closed nature of these worlds; communication is impossible when Caddy who is central to all three means something different to each." Benjy associates her with the smell of trees, Quentin with honor, and Jason with money. This closed world of the first three sections gradually moves into the open or public world when the conflict between Miss Quentin and Jason over money matters spills over into the life of Jefferson and the neighboring community of Mattson (significant in itself in that the constricting, confining, and protecting boundaries of Jefferson have been penetrated for the very first time). The private world of the Compsons has been exposed by this conflict, by Dilsey's emergence from the Compson house (itself a symbol, almost like Hawthorne's "House of the Seven Gables," of isolation) to go to Easter Sunday church service, and by the "outsider," the third-person narrator. Gradual progression from the private to the public world is marked, Olga Vickery observes, "by a corresponding shift in the form of apprehension": Benjy — uncommunicable sensations; Quentin — abstractions rather than sensations; Jason — logic and reason.

ORDERING OF SECTIONS. If *The Sound and The Fury* is the story of Benjy, Quentin, Jason, and Dilsey, on the Easter Days of 1928, then the *chronologues* have a point in insisting that the four sections should have been arranged in chronological order. Each of the four sections is clearly dated, and in chronological sequence would appear as follows: (1) Quentin's, dated June 2, 1910; (2) Jason's, April 6, 1928; (3) Benjy's, April 7, 1928; and (4) Dilsey's, April 8, 1928. Obviously, the reader would most certainly find Benjy's section much easier to read if it were to follow Jason's section, with its relatively straightforward prose language. The usual justification for the order as given (and which we have defended or explicated to some extent above) is that Benjy's section contains most of the scenes and themes that receive further development in the sections that follow. This is not quite accurate, Edmund Volpe argues. The Damuddy death scene, for example, which takes up so much of Benjy's section is referred to only twice and very briefly in Quentin's section. The long scene in which the idiot's name is changed from Maury to Benjamin in the first section occurs only once in Quentin's recollections (though, in all fairness, the change in name is alluded to constantly). Sections I and III share the scene in which Mr. Compson's funeral is described by Jason, but with little reference material taken from Benjy's section. "The thoughts of the three brothers," Volpe observes, "have many references in common, but the scenes that Benjy recalls are hardly essential to an understanding of the following sections."

Are we to conclude, then, that Faulkner's ordering of the sections was both whimsical and capricious? By no means; the arrangement is structurally justified because *The Sound and The Fury* is the story of the Compson family, *a story that covers a period in time from 1898 through the flight of Caddy's daughter, Quentin, from the Compson mansion in 1928.* Benjy's section thus serves to provide essential details of the early childhood and adolescence of the four Compson children (and allegorically, perhaps, of the whole Compson clan back to its very beginnings). Quentin's section hardly touches upon these early scenes; rather, his thoughts are centered upon the events of the summer of 1909 (and allegorically, perhaps, represent the Compson clan's first testing of its basic ideals). Jason in his section briefly recalls only one incident preceding Mr. Compson's funeral in 1912: the time Mrs. Compson put on mourning clothes because Caddy was kissed by a boy (the beginning of the decline and fall of the Compson clan?). The final section (Dilsey's and the author's) covers the year 1928 exclusively.

The four sections taken together tell the story of the Compson family (actually the last generation of the Compson clan; *The Sound and The Fury* is merely one part of the total Compson — or Sartoris, or Southern — saga which Faulkner was presenting *in his total work* in a literary-historical perspective); arrangement of the sections, Volpe concludes, "is therefore chronological, logical, and unalterable. In a Faulkner novel, structure and theme are inseparable."

TIME, THEME, AND STRUCTURE. "Throughout *The Sound and The Fury*," Perrin Lowrey observes, "clocks and watches and references to time provide a ticking refrain to the central action. . . . Each of [the major characters] holds an idea of time which is appropriate to the theme which Faulkner wishes to express and which serves the total structure he has created as well. . . . In the final structure the characters' time concepts are correlated artistically with the various time devices which serve the telling of the story. . . ."

The two distinctly different action lines cover two distinctly different time spans. The first and more apparent action line covers events which take place on April 6, 7, and 8 in 1928, and concerns the conflict between Jason and Miss Quentin. The larger, more inclusive action line begins in 1898, when the Compson children were small, and ends on April 8, 1928; in short, *the* story line of *The Sound and The Fury*, as indicated above. As Faulkner saw it, if there were two distinctly different (but not mutually exclusive) action lines, there should of necessity be two different ways of treating the overall action. For example, if the latter action line as described above is the *major* one, then the three-day action covered in sections I, III, and IV must be considered subordinate to the major action line covering all the important events that have happened in the Compson family over a whole generation (1898 to 1928), and as a climax serving in turn as a special device to get the whole story told. The device, a kind of remembrance-of-things-past technique, was particularly essential because the author placed so much more importance on the past than on the present. The novel represents not so much a search for identity (if at all) as a search for origins. Hence, *we may refer to this work as a "psychohistorical" novel.* In another sense, then, the novel, though at first reading apparently chaotic, is actually more chronologically structured (within Faulkner's objectives) than thought to be at first.

STRUCTURE AND MUSIC. The structure of *The Sound and The Fury* has lent itself to all sorts of analogies. To the French critic, Maurice Coindreau, *The Sound and The Fury* is a "demoniac symphony" lacking only the gaiety of a scherzo. He sees Faulkner as essentially musical in his approach to the structuring of the novel, with Faulkner using the system of themes, not in the manner of a fugue in which one simple theme develops and undergoes all sorts of variations, but employing multiple themes "which start out, vanish, and reappear to disappear again until the moment they sound forth in all their richness. . . ." Coindreau labels the sections in his extremely impressionistic interpretation as follows: Benjy's section — *Moderato;* Quentin's section — *Adagio;* Jason's section — *Allegro;* the fourth section — *Andante religioso, Allegro furioso, Allegro barbaro,* and *Lento.* It must be left to the reader to decide whether this musical analogy is a help or a hindrance in comprehending the structure of the novel.

THE SOUND AND THE FURY AS FAMILY CHRONICLE. More helpful by any standard is Hyatt H. Waggoner's comparison of this novel with other examples of nineteenth-century fiction, with James Joyce, and then with itself as a novel *sui generis*. In this story of a family over a period of about thirty years, Waggoner sees similarities between *The Sound and The Fury* and *David Copperfield* or *Henry Esmond,* rather than with James Joyce's *Ulysses.* Although the manner of telling the story is different, the story itself is concerned with the basics of birth, death, marriage, and death again. In *Ulysses,* Joyce uses familiar, trivial events as catalysts or evokers of echoes and allusions; in *The Sound and The Fury,* the events themselves carry their own significance. It is the *manner* of telling the story that distracts our attention from the fairly familiar and commonplace story itself. If this same story were recast in a different narrative form, the story "would serve for a traditional, pre-Joycean novel. That they [the events] are *not* told in that manner is of course of the essence. . . ." (We shall discuss Faulkner's narrative technique in greater detail below.)

FROM CONCRETE TO ABSTRACT. *The Sound and The Fury* may or may not be essentially an old-fashioned Christian novel telling a tale (or parable) of the innocence of an idiot (Benjy) and a Negro woman (Dilsey) "interrupted" by a neurotic romantic who had lost all faith (Quentin) and a worldly pragmatist who had sold his heritage for a mess of pottage (Jason). Waggoner analyzes the manner of telling this familiar story as follows: The novel moves from the concrete to the abstract in several ways. It moves from Benjy, held in by time only because he is incapable of abstract thinking; to Quentin, who seeks to escape from the constrictions of time through abstractions, but can find that final release only in death; to Jason, who is preoccupied with the concrete moment and its "practical realities," money and power, which in the final analysis are abstractions as forceful and compelling as Quentin's "honor"; to Dilsey, who accepts the final abstraction, timeless faith, which "enables her to live in time and deal with concrete experience without frustration and without despair. . . ."

STRUCTURE AND THEME ARE ONE. This is the critical

"motto" of the book. Both theme and structure, Waggoner suggests, "assert the possibility of achieving a difficult order out of the chaotic flux of time." All the Compsons in the end fall victims to that difficult order, mainly because "the saving positive values, the ordering beliefs, are embodied here in an idiot and in a representative of an ignorant and despised people." By the end of the novel, the irony of the title becomes evident. Benjy the idiot has turned out to be the carrier of those values we have come to accept, and the tale he tells "signifies much, and if one of its meanings is that life is at last 'a stalemate of dust and desire,' it is only one, and not the one that the idiot himself suggests to us." But Benjy is just one of the two ends of the thematic, structural, and narrative nexus of the novel; there is also Dilsey, who in her innocence and ignorance continues to live, to *endure* through a "foolishness" called faith by *all* the Jasons in this world.

NARRATIVE, STRUCTURE, AND THEME. It is very unlikely that the argument over Faulkner's non-chronological arrangement of the four sections of *The Sound and The Fury* will ever be satisfactorily settled. Nor will the large majority of the critics ever agree on reasons for Faulkner's having placed the Benjy section first, for having assigned what is probably the crucial, seminal section of the novel to an idiot, and for having chosen to use *four* different types of narrative technique. Therefore, *we shall attempt to show that,* if structure and theme are almost inseparable in a Faulkner novel, and that narrative technique is often an integral part of structure in a Faulkner novel, then *Faulkner had no other literary or esthetic choice in the narrative techniques employed* in *The Sound and The Fury.*

SECTION I — BENJY. *The Sound and The Fury* may safely be assumed to be a novel about disorder, decay and disintegration, and little or no perspective (the theme, or one of the major themes?). If so, then the flat, perspectiveless language assigned to Benjy is most appropriate to establish that theme. Moreover, the events in the early years of the four main characters (Benjy, Caddy, Quentin, and Jason) definitely foreshadow many of the key events in the later years of these same four characters. For example, when Caddy reaches early womanhood, she *soils* her honor with a *stain* that will not come off. (This is foreshadowed by the muddy drawers of young Caddy. When Dilsey discovers the mudstain on Caddy's backside, she tries to clean it off, but can't.) Quentin, the self-appointed custodian of family honor, later tries to remove that same "stain" from the family honor by committing suicide. Jason capitalizes on Caddy's dishonor (and the by-product thereof, Miss Quentin) by blackmailing his sister for all he can get.

Still another childhood situation or characteristic is used to foreshadow later events. Jason even as a child has the habit of walking with his hands in his pockets ("holding his money," perhaps?) and is cautioned to carry his hands and arms free so as not to fall down, as he often does. Later on, he "holds his money" (real money, this time) by keeping it in his room locked in a box instead of in a bank. He is subsequently robbed of this money by his niece, Miss Quentin, who then runs off with the carnival man.

RAMBLING WITH BENJY. Faulkner did not use the conventional devices of the stream-of-consciousness technique (cf. Joyce, Woolf, Evelyn Scott, *et al*) to signal transitions between thoughts (though he does so in Section II, however) ; instead, for Benjy, the reader is given external physical clues to signify a transition in thought. Sometimes *italic type* is used to indicate a shift from the present to the past, or from one recalled scene to another; it is not, however, a consistently reliable guide. (At one time Faulkner contemplated having the various sections printed in different colors of ink, to help the reader.) Another clue to a shift in scene and to the time sequence of events in the story is given by Benjy's Negro caretakers, "nurses," or companions — Versh, T. P., and Luster. *For almost every scene set in the present*

(April 7, 1928), *the reader should look for the name of Luster, Dilsey's youngest child; for scenes from the past, the name of Versh or T. P.* These three Negro characters also indicate the approximate time that an event takes place: Benjy as a child is watched over by Versh; at eleven, T. P. becomes his caretaker-companion; in early manhood, Luster takes charge of him.

FIFTEEN KEY EVENTS. Benjy relives or reconstructs fifteen key events from the past, many of them presented in short fragments or units in a sequence. A number of these events are presented in closely spaced fragments and can be followed fairly easily; but other events are broken up into episodes and are then scattered throughout the section. To recognize the relationship between fragments, Faulkner has provided some clues, much as the presence of certain characters in certain situations, or the repetition of key words. Caddy's wedding scene is recalled in a fragment, for example, every time T. P. uses the words "whooey" or "sasprilluh."

Moreover, every line in the Benjy section (with a few exceptions such as "Caddy smelled like trees") is identifiable either as part of one of the fifteen key events or scenes recalled by Benjy, or as part of the action in the present. Some of the remembered scenes are long, and justifiably so because of their extreme importance to the theme. Mention has repeatedly been made in this discussion of Damuddy's death scene in which Caddy and her brothers *establish* the basis for most of the action to come, or for that matter, for the whole book itself. This scene has eighteen fragments scattered throughout the section. The scene in which Benjy's name is changed (from Maury to Benjamin), although not as pivotal a scene, has twenty separate fragments. In general, most of the scenes are short, and *their* fragments are not scattered too far afield.

SECTION II — QUENTIN. The opening pages of this sec-

tion leave the reader with the impression that thoughts flash-
ing through Quentin's mind (in stream-of-consciousness fashion) are as disconnected as those in motion in Benjy's mind.
But there is a difference: Quentin's thoughts are all interrelated. Moreover, the language of his thoughts is neither
as flat nor as perspectiveless as Benjy's. Quentin thinks in
abstractions and symbols (and it is his section that provides
the reader with the major proportion of the symbolism in
the novel). However, because his is a disturbed, obsessed
mind, the reader should expect all his thoughts, images,
memories, and responses to immediate stimuli to be related
to his obsession (with honor, with Caddy's loss of virginity
and innocence). Associations from the present are bound to
stimulate his memories, and in due time the sequence of
events that have driven him to suicide is unfolded. (The
reader would do well — and simultaneously entertain himself — by trying to anticipate the author by identifying
these events for himself.) Quentin is, by all quasi-psychiatric
standards, a pre-psychotic, and as such cannot or will not
comprehend the real significance of his memories; instead,
he will evaluate them — and so should the reader — in their
proper (that is, abnormal) perspective.

SECTION III — JASON. Jason is a *normal* bastard. One
should, therefore, not attempt to confuse morality with mentality. His tastes and desires may be amoral (very infre-
quently, immoral), but however one appraises his mad rages
of greed and frustration, his thought-pattern is logical, and
so is his language. The section is set in the form of an interior
monologue, but there is none of the rambling, free-associational thinking of Benjy or Quentin in his piece. Moreover,
because he is unlearned, egotistical, and obvious, his thoughts
are easy to follow. And so we learn from his own thoughts
*and words* (the reader should note very carefully how the
language has "surfaced" by the time the third section is
reached) that unlike Quentin he has striven to cut himself
off from the past. When he does recall a few scenes from the
past, they are registered in his mind in the present (or what

some grammarians would call the *historical present*) : "she says, I says," etc. In the main, Jason as man and thinker, prefers to live in the present, the immediate present of April 6, 1928.

**SECTION IV — DILSEY.** Most of the third-person narrative in this section centers around Dilsey, Faulkner's "proxy," as it were. Faulkner uses her to narrate the closing events in the Compson story (that is, until the Appendix came out in 1946), and to provide a conclusion and a thematic counterpoint to the preceding sections. The story also had to be rounded out by coming full circle, from Benjy to Dilsey, from innocence to innocence. And, finally, Faulkner once again proves that theme, structure, and narrative technique are all interrelated.

**MAJOR THEMES OF *THE SOUND AND THE FURY*.** "The novel dramatizes a deterioration from the past to the present," says Edmund Volpe. "A tragic sense of loss is so predominant and pervasive in each section and in almost every scene, that it can be considered the basic theme of the novel — a theme similar to that of Eliot's 'The Waste Land.' " If Volpe is right and if that is the *major* theme of the novel, then it is much too large a theme to be considered by itself; other themes must be subsumed under it — modern life as a "paradise lost," or loss of innocence; life as a tale signifying nothing; man, if he is to survive, must endure. Let us examine the Faulkner-Eliot theme first.

**MODERN LIFE AS A WASTE LAND.** Both Eliot and Faulkner see modern society as materialistic and commercialized, where humanistic values have been routed by values of the marketplace and the countinghouse. In one sense, man has reverted to the Ptolemaic concept of the geocentric or egocentric universe in which man in his self-centeredness has rejected all the restraints, inhibitions, traditions, and values of the past for a patently finite, sterile existence. Both Eliot and Faulkner make use of the past to reveal the aimlessness and sterility of the present. Eliot, for his part, relies on historical or literary contrasts to evoke those specific (but universal) values man respected in the past: the meaningful, effectual rituals of primitive society (all over the world) in contrast to the meaningless, sham rituals of modern society; in fact, the disappearance of ritual (both spiritual and sociological) from modern life altogether. Without ceremony (especially the "ceremony of innocence," in Yeats's phrase, or faith), Eliot says, along with Yeats, "things fall apart."

Faulkner, for his part, makes use of the past (and a more parochial one at that) in a far less specific way; his values (according to some critics) are those of ante-bellum Southern society, particularly in *The Sound and The Fury*. But Faulkner is not really that parochial; there is very little evidence in the novel itself of a nostalgic longing for the specific values of that time in Southern history. When Quentin vaguely refers to the values of a plantation society, it is only because he is actually a "romantic adolescent," rather than a Southern reactionary trying to turn back the clock to a self-contained, closed society completely insulated from all historical, social, and economic forces. For Quentin, the present, to be sure, appears to be a waste land, but the past that he (and Faulkner) longs for is not that distant past but the immediate past — "the world of childhood, innocent and idealistic. . . ." One need but juxtapose the idyllic childhood of the Compson brothers and sister with their present life to feel and experience the deterioration, decay, and loss that modern life (in particular their generation — and Faulkner's) has bestowed upon them. And yet, as powerful as that theme may be, it derives most of its force from its applicability, not merely to the Compsons, one family, but to a much larger segment of humanity, and thus becomes, like Eliot's poem, a metaphor for the spiritual crisis of modern man.

MODERN LIFE AS PARADISE LOST. The first three sections represent a thematic progression of man through the different stages of his development. Benjy's is the child's stage; Quentin's, the adolescent's; Jason's the cocksure, egotistical adult's. Benjy's is the most important because he represents original innocence in the Garden of Eden. He is Adam before the apple was eaten — sterile and sexless, an idiot, and therefore the first individual, the first *private* citizen (see the dictionary definition of the Greek word *idiotes*), all feeling, innocent of any guile, able to talk to the animals (but not in *human* language) with his blabbering and bellowing. He is all feeling and no reason — man's first (and perhaps only) blissful state. As the progression moves from Benjy to Quentin, there is a marked loss of feeling as abstract thinking takes over. Deterioration in emotional response eventually finds its bottom in the triumph of reason over feeling in the character of Jason. Benjy's world is the child's world (man-as-child world) — secure, orderly, and full of love. But as he remembers each scene, there is a progressive loss of these values, culminating in the one great loss of his whole existence — his sister Caddy. And, we may add, in her full name, *Candace*, we may recognize a cognate of *candid*, meaning free, open, frank, almost innocent. Benjy, Quentin, and Faulkner himself, all lament that "paradise lost," innocence. Moreover, it is probably Quentin who feels most responsible for this loss when he remarks, (recollecting) "Let us sell Benjy's pasture so that Quentin may go to Harvard. . . . I have sold Benjy's pasture and I can be dead in Harvard." (216-217)

MODERN LIFE AS A TALE SIGNIFYING NOTHING. Benjy's section introduces this theme, along with its counterpart: the *negative* status of meaning in modern experience, loss and absence; the *positive* status of meaning, presence and endurance. Benjy's section gives focus to neither one. Quentin's section attempts to establish the reality of the second (or positive) part of the theme, but succeeds only in affirming the first part. Jason's section, through dramatic irony, affirms the negative status of meaning. Dilsey's section successfully draws both parts into focus, and the second part (the *positive* status of meaning) emerges as dominant. Dilsey and her kind will endure; others, who have the same innocence (or ignorance, another form of innocence), the same feeling, but not the same faith, will be confined, destroyed, or will destroy themselves.

But despite Dilsey's affirmation of the *positive* status of meaning, one must take into account the abrupt shift that occurs in both the character of the narrator and the narrative technique in Jason's section. His is the voice of the future, of all the Snopeses to come, and it is this realization of what life is beginning to mean and will mean that transcends any glorious hopes we (and Faulkner) may have that the Dilseys will triumph. In the Jason section there is a definite shift in emphasis from the *loss* of meaning to the *complete absence* of all meaning.

TO SUFFER IS TO ENDURE. "Faulkner's great subject," Allen Tate has observed, ". . . is passive suffering, the victim being destroyed either by society or by dark forces within himself. Faulkner is one of the great exemplars of the international school of fiction which for more than a century has reversed the Aristotelian doctrine that tragedy is an action, not a quality." If Tate is to be taken at his word, the temptation is then very great to call the whole Compson clan tragic, the whole South tragic, and perhaps all of the United States tragic. At least so far as socialization has deprived man of much of his freedom, whether it be through surrender to a multiplicity of laws, or to empty rituals and meaningless relationships, then we are all tragic victims, Northerners and Southerners. If we are to attribute a tragic quality to the consequence resulting from a loss of the wilderness, that second-chance Eden — be it through sale of Benjy's pasture to get Quentin to the "think tanks" of Harvard, or through Jason's readiness to break up a Georgian Manse and sell the pieces as ramshackle bungalows, or through pollution of forest lands and streams, despoliation of virgin timber, and asphaltization of greenbelts — we are all once again victims, Northerners and Southerners. But the truly tragic figure in *The Sound and The Fury* is Quentin, who is indeed a prisoner of the past (individually and as a symbol of all the Compsons), a Southerner more sensitive than any other Southerner to the South's guilt for what it has done to the Negroes, and a man shut off from the wholesome forces of nature by his own moral inhibitions and the inhibiting scruples of Southern Puritanism. It is this "virgin suicide" who suffers most because of his sensitivity, but who cannot find strength to endure because he has lost all faith in man, nature, and God. *If* Benjy suffers, he is at the same time insulated by his mental incompetence; he has no way of knowing it; he is even impervious to most physical pain, as in the episode wherein he touches the hot stove. Jason does not suffer because he refuses to suffer. Who steals his purse, steals everything. Emotionally and spiritually, the man is intact. Caddy rejects suffering by running away from it, followed in time by her daughter, Miss Quentin. Mrs. Compson sublimates her suffering in neurotic fantasies. Mr. Compson dissolves his suffering in drinking.

Only Dilsey suffers, recognizes it, accepts it as part of life and nature, and thus endures. She is neither tragic nor heroic; she is human. For her, every day is Easter Sunday: nothing really dies, resurrection is all. From Benjy to Dilsey, from one innocence to another, *The Sound and the Fury* is the tale of what man has done to man.

STYLE—JUXTAPOSITION, REPETITION, AND SYMBOLS. Outstanding examples of Faulkner's elegant, complex, and "peculiar" style are to be found in Quentin's section. Cumulative thematic implications appear there in their most concentrated form, and are produced through juxtaposition, repetition, and implied association or contrast. The same technique, however, is used in other sections, too, mainly to reinforce the structure of the entire novel. With some help from the author, the reader moves slowly (sometimes painfully) from concrete experiences or events to complex implications, from confusion to a gradually evolving understanding. There is, after all, no simple meaning for the Compson world, and Faulkner offers no meaning, even in the final section of the novel (at least not in his own voice). Since he is the objective "outsider," figurative language is used sparingly, even as a convenient evasion of the prohibition against "editorializing."

Let us examine some choicer examples of juxtaposition, etc. Jason may damn the "redneck" farmers of Jefferson, even after he has just defended them. Caroline Compson will constantly complain about her physical and familial burdens, but Dilsey will be carrying the full weight of the family's responsibilities. By allowing the "streams of consciousness" of Benjy and Quentin to arrange data by free association rather than by external chronology, Faulkner produces compressed juxtapositions that serve to reveal characteristics of both minds and thus suggest the larger themes of the novel. By interweaving Benjy's memories of Caddy's wedding with his own memories of four deaths (Damuddy's, Quentin's, Mr. Compson's, and Roskus's), Faulkner suggests the *common denominator of loss* in all five events. Finally, by interconnecting Quentin's affair with the little Italian girl and his memories of childhood activities with Caddy, Faulkner suggests not only Quentin's obsessions (see section on symbolism below for an expansion of this point), but a world outside the Compson family that may share many of that family's dilemmas. And this footnote: by placing much of the action of the Quentin section up north, Faulkner achieves an impressive contrast between the "closed" world of the South and the (relatively) open world of the North. Again, in the Jason section, by having Jason pursue Miss Quentin out of Jefferson into Mattson, Faulkner once again provides a contrast between the small world of the Compsons (in Jefferson) and the "modern" world outside Jefferson.

STYLE—REPETITION AND SYMBOLS. Although Benjy, of necessity, speaks in short, simple sentences almost completely devoid of figurative language, such remarks as "Caddy smelled like trees" (almost a "motto" or recurrent simile), however, do take on larger meaning later on. Jason's diction, on the other hand, is for the most part both informal (even downright uninhibited) and aphoristic. His section opens with the terse phrase, "Once a bitch, always a bitch," and the reader immediately knows who will be the object of his disaffection. His language is contemporary, full of slang, colloquial or earthy similes redolent of the marketplace or the "redneck" farm, and sarcastic understatement or hyperbole characteristic of the frontier rather than of the town. His is a clever mind clearly reflecting in his language the "prejudices of his day and the conventions of a bitter and narrow materialism."

Quentin's mind is more unstable than Benjy's; that is, it not only shifts more often than Benjy's (about 200 times as compared to about 100 times in Benjy's section) but also often thinks, not in simple, *complete* sentences but in sentence fragments. He is, after all, in quite a mental frenzy on that fateful June day, and counterpoints the seemingly controlled physical actions of that day with obsessively repeated key scenes or even phrases from his past. What do these compulsive repetitions indicate? Very likely the way in which Quentin is "fusing widely varying experiences to conform to the rigid pattern of his obsessions." Similar fusing tendencies, this time expressed through symbolic and metaphorical language, appear most characteristically in the scene (p. 149) in which Quentin has just left the bridge from which three boys have been trying, unsuccessfully, to catch an enormous trout. Special note should be taken of the ways in which the water and the sun's rays evoke image after image.

LANGUAGE. During the February 20, 1957 session at the University of Virginia, Faulkner was asked why, in the last part of the Quentin section, capitals on names and on the pronoun "I" began to disappear. Faulkner's answer was that Quentin was a dying man, already practically out of life, and that "those things that were important in life don't mean anything to him anymore." At a later session, another student complained that Faulkner seemed to show a cavalier disregard for subjects and predicates with verbs "and all those things." The reference was originally to the language in the Benjy section, and so Faulkner's "defense" went thus: "I was trying to tell this story as it seemed to me that idiot child saw it. And that idiot child to me didn't know what a question, what an interrogation was. He didn't know too much about grammar, he spoke only through his senses."

HOW AN IDIOT THINKS. How does an idiot *talk?* He babbles, grunts, groans, whines, bellows, etc. How does an idiot *think?* No one really knows, except that his thoughts are even more fragmented and incoherent than Benjy's, and consequently Faulkner's version of an idiot's thought processes, although an *approximation,* becomes acceptable to the reader through the language used to report Benjy's "flow of memory." As an artist, Faulkner is, after all, concerned not so much with the mental life of Benjy as with the attempt to render a *plausible* effect — "a flow of disturbed memory which, in the absence of contrary knowledge, can be associated with an idiot." Faulkner asks the reader to assume that this disturbed flow of memory makes some sense and follows some primitive kind of order, although the reader's first impression is that Benjy's memories are inchoate. To sustain that impression, Faulkner assigns to Benjy's thoughts or memories a minimum of rhetoric, a simple syntax, and a grammatical monotony composed of short declarative sentences rather than complex sentences built on logic, subordination, qualification, and sequence. Monotony, although inherent in such a commitment to primitive diction, is skillfully interrupted by frequent time shifts, concrete pictorial images, and many sharply inflected voices. The effect, Irving Howe notes, is that "The internal regularity of individual sentences is thus played off against the subtle pacing and tonal variety of the sequence as a whole — the sentences invoking Benjy and the sequence that which exists beyond Benjy." Though the rhythm and form of the sentences are fixed, the tempo is varied by introduction first of relatively large units conveying Benjy's memories, then small fragments, and, at the climax, very short sentences excitedly calling up a crazy quilt of memories going back to 1898, 1910, and 1928, but not necessarily in that chronological order. The flow of memory finally comes to a stop with Benjy's strongest memories, those of his childhood. Unlike the language in Quentin's section, Benjy's "thought language" contains few similes or metaphors (he is, of course, incapable of abstract language), but many concrete nouns naming common objects, and simple adjectives referring to blunt sensations (of which he has many). These nouns and adjectives serve Faulkner's main artistic intention — to establish transitions in time. Benjy must be stimulated, even prodded, to move from one track of memory to another, and the stimuli come in the form of places, names, smells, and feelings. And, as in many other parts of the novel, meanings Faulkner intends to convey are underscored by association, incongruity, and juxtaposition. Through these devices, the past becomes simultaneous with the present, meanings acquire symbolic overtones, and the net effect is one of pathos, sadness, loss, and more loss.

SYMBOLISM. We have already seen that there are few symbols in the Benjy section, and these symbols, because they are inherent in the action itself, seem natural, organic, spontaneous, and expected. With the Quentin section, however, Faulkner the reluctant symbolist, really goes to town. Quentin's greater sensitivity and introspectiveness, as well as his basically romantic temperament, provide Faulkner with reasons for scattering symbols far and wide throughout Quentin's reconstruction of the past. Symbolic patterns appear throughout the novel, but the richest and most provocative ones occur in the Quentin section. In that section alone, water as a symbol appears 61 times; shadow, 53; door, 34; sister, 30; honeysuckle, 27; and innumerable references to time (Quentin's watch, the Harvard chimes, and all sorts of clocks). *Numerically, water is the predominant symbol, and properly so, since the section will end with Quentin's suicide by drowning.* Water for Quentin (and for Faulkner, and, incidentally, for T. S. Eliot in "The Waste Land") had psychological and mythic implications as the unconscious; it likewise suggested to Quentin death and rebirth, and in drowning himself, he at last achieved escape through a "final ritualistic purification."

"LIFE'S BUT A WALKING SHADOW . . ." Shadow as symbol or motif, however, though slightly less predominant than water, suggests a greater variety of meanings than do all the others. The association which first comes to mind — and Faulkner might very well have chosen for the title the line, "Life's but a walking shadow, etc.," from the same Shakespearean passage (*Macbeth*, V, v) in which he found the title, "The Sound and The Fury" (. . . It is a tale/ Told by an idiot, full of sound and fury,/ Signifying nothing . . .) — is metaphorical and philosophical. A second association is the religious one: "Yea, though I walk through the valley of the shadow of death . . ." (*Psalm* 23). Still a third association comes to mind: the shadows in Plato's Cave (*The Republic*, Book VII), symbolic of the illusions which man in his ignorance mistakes for reality. Quentin could very well have been preoccupied with those shadows in the cave, even as he was eternally confused by the metaphysical distinction between illusion and reality; or, more specifically in his case, between life *as it is* and life *as he would have it*, or *as it seems to have been* in a pre-twentieth-century, aristocratic South. "He is a romantic," Louise Dauner observes, "beset by the growing crudities of a naturalistic culture." ("Naturalistic" or "materialistic"? Faulkner himself seemed to be harking back to the "naturalism" of "The Bear," among other works.)

SHADOW AS "DARK BROTHER." For the first half of the Quentin section, shadow frequently serves as a literal time and space signal, or as a "bridge" between some object or element and his obsession with Caddy (pp. 100, 101, 166, 173). But it is the association of shadow with time, Quentin's greatest enemy, that provides the reader with the largest number of implications. Time, marked by the movement of the sun through the day, evokes the theme of self-punishment, and the shadow (the sun's "dark brother") becomes Quentin's own shadow (he is continually stepping on his own shadow), which thus assumes meaning as the Double, the alter ego, the "dark brother" (p. 153). Quentin is continually stepping on his own shadow, as if he wished to injure or destroy his shadow, or wickeder self. Faulkner may be suggesting here that the shadow is the soul, the connoter of immortality, and to injure or lose this immortal part of man is to invite illness or death (pp. 109, 114).

JUNGIAN ARCHETYPE. Carrying the concept of the shadow as the opposing self one step further, the Jungian Shadow archetype may be applied to Quentin's preoccupation with shadows. According to Jung, the Shadow is the repressed, inferior, or darker aspect of the psyche; in Quentin's case, that part of him which lusts incestuously for Caddy and which must be destroyed (not repressed anymore) through the ultimate form of self-punishment — suicide. Try as he may, Quentin's psychic immaturity and disunity prevent him from reconciling his real(?) self with his darker aspect, the process that Jung calls "the integration with the Shadow." The shadow, as an archetypal symbol, therefore, tells the reader a great deal about Quentin, and also why he *had* to commit suicide.

Before Quentin finally opts for suicide, he suggests a mutual death pact to Caddy (p. 176) as a way in which both may find release from their obsessions (Caddy apparently reciprocates Quentin's desire for her) and their guilt feelings (Quentin assumes Caddy feels as strongly about loss of her virginity as he does). In this remembered scene, the shadows represent the completely obsessed Quentin — with Caddy, who suggests sex; with sex, which suggests death; with death, which is implied in the deterioration of the family itself, in the death of the noble traditions of the past, and in the decadent values of the present. For Quentin, existence has become a reverse Coleridgean process: *death-in-life*. Shadow has become substance.

More shadows, more forecasts of death may be found in Quentin's ride back from town to the Harvard Quadrangle on that last fateful day (p. 188). Twilight shadows epitomize his whole existence — vague, unreal, insubstantial, enigmatic, sterile, out of joint, out of time, more shadow than substance. He recalls the last words he had had with his father, and his father's trenchant comment: "you are not thinking of finitude you are contemplating an apotheosis in which a temporary state of mind will become symmetrical above the flesh it will not quite discard you will not even be dead . . ." Quentin is now convinced that the only way in which he can achieve this "apotheosis" is through suicide. He gets off the trolley, returns to his room, meticulously arranges his personal things, and leaves for the site of his escape and apotheosis — the amniotic waters of death. "Yea, though I walk in the valley of the shadow of death . . ." Finally, for Quentin more than for all the other characters, a memory is a *shadow* of an event, experience, or feeling.

HONEYSUCKLE, SEX, DEATH, PARADOX. Consider a paradox: Quentin desires death above everything else. Sex suggests death to him. Sex nauseates him. The honeysuckle symbolizes sex, and therefore disgusts him. Why does Quentin reject sex? First, simply and obviously, because as a good Southern Fundamentalist he must think of it as something dirty and unholy, to be associated eternally with Original Sin, the Fall of Man, the Old Adam, etc. But sex is also the generative force in reproduction, and herein we come to the crux of the matter. Quentin is a prisoner of the past, an

unwilling occupant of the present, and a man absolutely
uninterested in the future. Or, as Sartre said, for Quentin
there is no future. Why then, Quentin asks, should I contribute young human beings to people a future that I do not
believe in? Quentin would have been happier if he had been
born a eunuch, devoid of all sexual feeling and desire. And
so, he rejects sex, even as it suggests (spiritual) death to
him. Moreover, he is repelled by whatever symbolizes sex to
him — Caddy, mud (muddy drawers), honeysuckle, etc.

"I HAD TO PANT TO GET ANY AIR AT ALL . . ." Honeysuckle is probably the most important single image in the
Quentin section. It is associated with water or wetness (rain,
drizzle, mist) since the smell of the flower hangs heavily in
the wet atmosphere, especially in the crucial hog wallow (a
value judgment? anti-sex? "dirty"?) and suicide pact scenes
with Caddy. Honeysuckle also suggests or recalls images
of sex and death, of shadow, twilight, grayness, Benjy's bellowing, Caddy's marriage, etc. And Quentin says, "I had to
pant to get any air at all out of that thick gray honeysuckle"
(p. 170).

SOME MINOR SYMBOLS. Water, shadow, and honeysuckle (a correlate of water) are the major symbols or
motifs in the novel. There are a few other symbols that bear
some discussion, since they are an integral part of Faulkner's
quasi-poetic style. There is the GULL, associated by Quentin's father with time (and death) : "time is your misfortune
Father said. A gull on an invisible wire attached through
space dragged" (p. 123). The GOLF COURSE, formerly the
Compson pasture, represents the fatal mistake the family
made by selling off part of its heritage : "let us sell Benjy's
pasture so that Quentin may go to Harvard," Quentin recol-
lects (p. 216). The CADDY, associated with the golf course,
but a double reminder to Benjy of what he has lost: the pasture and his *sister* Caddy (short for Candace; Mrs. Compson never used the short form). The color RED, as in the

symbolizes illicit passion for Jason: "The fire was in her eyes and on her mouth. Her mouth was red" (p. 82). For Quentin, the symbol of illicit passion or sex is MUD. He says: *"She hit my hands away I smeared mud on her with the other hand I couldn't feel the wet smacking of her hand I wiped mud from my legs smeared it in her wet hard turning body . . ."* (p. 170). This is sex for Quentin — wallowing in the mud. GASOLINE calls up several associations; with fuel for automobiles, with a cleanser (to remove the bloodstain from Quentin's vest, for example), with Jason's intolerance of the smell of gasoline, with Jason's disapproval of the sale of the Benjy pasture in order to send Quentin to Harvard, and with gasoline as a *modern* fuel for *modern* motor cars (so many things modern were distasteful to Quentin) (p. 213). Quentin received the bloodstain on his vest in the fight with Julio, the little Italian girl's brother. The FIGHT becomes a symbol of Quentin's failure to protect and save *his* sister Caddy from dishonor (Julio of course suspected Quentin of trying to seduce his little sister), a failure which contributed so much to the sense of guilt that eventually sent Quentin to his suicide. And, finally, Caddy names her illegitimate child QUENTIN, after her brother. Her mother had also named her youngest son (later called Benjy) Maury, after *her* brother. Perhaps it was only custom to do so, but it is possible to construe that gesture as a "consummation" of the incest that Caddy desired and offered to, but did not commit, with Quentin.

SYMBOL-MONGERING. Before continuing to list other symbols in the novel, let us take note of a serious *caveat* that Cleanth Brooks provides. "This misplaced stress upon realism might seem to find its proper corrective in a compensating stress upon symbolism," he writes, "—not facts but what they point to, not Faulkner as a sociologist but Faulkner as a symbolist poet." To Brooks (and to Faulkner himself, as we shall see in a moment), the overcompensating critics have been guilty of "symbol-mongering" — which Brooks defines as "something morbid, excessive, and obsessed, a grotesque red tie worn by the man who runs off with Miss Quentin, parody of anything like an adequate, careful reading."

Faulkner himself said in answer to a question concerning the symbolic meaning of the dates in *The Sound and The Fury* that "it was quite instinctive that I picked out Easter, that I wasn't writing any symbolism of the Passion Week at all. I just — that was a tool that was good for the particular corner I was going to turn in my chicken-house and so I used it." He also said that the shadow was not a deliberate symbolism, but then went on to say that that "shadow that stayed on his mind so much was foreknowledge of his own death . . . Death is here, shall I step into it, or shall I step away from it a little longer? I won't escape it, but shall I accept it now or shall I put it off until next Friday? I think that if it had any reason that must have been it." Deliberate symbolism or not? The reader must decide for himself.

MORE SYMBOL-MONGERING. Despite Faulkner's disclaimer, the (hitherto reluctant, now) instinctive symbolist, and the *caveat* of Brooks, let's examine a few more examples of "symbol-mongering," some selected by Brooks, others selected by us.

Is there any *subtle* symbolic meaning in the name-changing scene? Benjy's mother is a vain and superficial woman who keeps asserting that the Bascombs are as good as the Compsons. But Maury Compson, idiot, is hardly a favorable reflection on Maury Bascomb and other Bascombs. So *Maury* Compson becomes *Benjamin* (Benjy) Compson, and thus no Bascomb genes have contributed to Benjamin's (she never uses the shorter name) idiocy. That's all there is to that, Brooks contends. But one critic has come up with the *real*, the symbolic meaning of the name-changing. The Compsons, he says are both primitive and superstitious, and evidently "assume that names have mysterious powers," and that *there is some sort of mysterious two-way street between a Maury Compson, idiot, and a Maury Bascomb, normal adult.* Still another critic takes the same scene one step further along the symbol path and claims that by removing her brother's name from her own son, Mrs. Compson is eliminating a possibly unconscious incestuous attraction to her brother. Furthermore, the critic asks, was Caddy repeating this same Freudian mistake in naming her child Quentin? Still another critic (the Freudian line, like the Banquo line, stretches out endlessly) sees no simple logic (the logic of tradition and custom) in the fact that Mrs. Compson's favorite son, Jason, has the same name as her husband (he dies in 1912), and that this poses another possible incestuous attachment, the repression of which is manifested by her neuroticism. How convincing a deduction can this be in the South where names are repeated unto the fourth generation? Jason Compson IV is to Jason Compson III (his father), Jason Compson II, and Jason Compson I as our own author, William Faulkner, is the fourth male in that family to carry the name of the original Colonel William Henry Faulkner. So much for the magic power of names.

But there is an even more startling bit of symbol-mongering that disturbs Brooks. It is the scene in which Quentin, deploring Caddy's loss of virginity to Dalton Ames, proposes that they join in a suicide pact. First he will kill her (suicide?), and then he will kill himself. He then takes out the knife and holds it to her throat. One critic has suggested that Quentin is "symbolically" (of course) about to perform a hysterectomy — that is, remove the "agent" of Caddy's (and the family's) dishonor. Brooks sees something far-fetched about representing Quentin as a kind of Jack the Ripper, and even more far-fetched in attempting such an operation *in the area of the throat.* (Without wishing to take sides at this point, one must advise Brooks that, according to Freud, such an anatomical displacement is fairly common. For example, in *The Merchant of Venice*, Shylock's demand for his pound of flesh from the region of Antonio's heart is really a desire to castrate him.) Better yet, another critic sees the knife in Quentin's hand as a symbolic penis; now,

Caddy's virginity having ceased to be a problem, Quentin feels less constrained to repress his incestuous desire for his sister.

We can offer no specific comment by Faulkner himself on the above examples, but it is interesting to note that the author did say (May 15, 1957, University of Virginia) that "the writer don't have to know Freud to have written things which anyone who does know Freud can divine and reduce into symbols. And so when the critic finds those symbols, they are of course there."

TIME CONCEPTS. The real subject of *The Sound and The Fury* is, according to Jean-Paul Sartre, man's unfortunate, submissive dependency on time. At first, the technique employed by Faulkner seems a negation of temporality (*timeness*), or more accurately, chronology; further examination proves it to be something more than that. For chronology is, after all, a system devised by man to measure time with clocks and calendars. To arrive at real time, however, man must discard such artificial measures which in effect don't measure at all. Primitive man measured time more realistically, not with calendars and clocks (although he did know about days, that is, courses of the sun, and moons, or what we call months) but in terms of work or distance traveled — a segment of time in which a field could be plowed, or a journey (cf. *jour*=day) from one point to another. In short, time was never an abstraction for him.

Faulkner's characters (as we shall see below) apparently negate time by measuring the past, not chronologically, but by reconstructing salient events. Their past is, says Sartre, "a matter of emotional constellations. Around a few central themes (Caddy's pregnancy, Benjy's castration, Quentin's suicide) gravitate innumerable silent masses." Therefore, how futile to rely on the absurd chronology of "the assertive and contradictory assurance" of the clock rather than on "the order of the heart."

Sartre also sees a close similarity between Faulkner's and Proust's concept of time. "The unspeakable present, leaking at every seam, those sudden invasions of the past, this emotional order, the opposite of the voluntary and intellectual order that is chronological but lacking in reality, these memories, these monstrous and discontinuous obsessions, these intermittencies of the heart — are not these reminiscent of the lost and recaptured time of Marcel Proust?" Yes and no. For Proust, salvation lay in time itself, in the complete *recapture* of the past. For Faulkner, the past was never completely forgotten or lost; the present was always threatened by "those sudden invasions of the past"; the past was an obsession.

The past likewise exerts so tremendous a pull on the present (in Faulkner's "metaphysics of time," as Sartre describes it) that the present can never move toward the future. Faulkner personally despairs of the future — any future — especially in this time of impossible and irresistible changes — cultural, political, economic, technological — and he is painfully aware of "our suffocation and a world dying of old age. I like his art," Sartre, the social and political activist concludes, "but I do not believe in his metaphysics. A closed future is still a future."

BENJY, UNCONSCIOUS OF TIME. Quentin best exemplifies Faulkner's "metaphysics of time"; for him there is no future, not even a "specious present"; reality *was* and *is* the past. Quentin is obsessed with time (see examples in section on symbolism above; other examples will follow below), but Benjy is absolutely unconscious of time. Because he cannot *conceive* of time, time does not *exist* for him. He can only experience sensation, and that only if it is momentary and fleeting. Even the present eludes him, since he is unaware of the passing of time; he lives in a past-present world. For a mind such as his, time or *timeness* does not exist, and so everything happens for him in dramatic terms *in the present*. (It might be more accurate, perhaps, if we may borrow a grammatical term, to call it the *historical present* — a past event described in the present tense.) And because there is no *conscious* past for Benjy, in his section the reader is given a *timeless* view of all the Compsons. Benjy's suspension of time permits Faulkner to place the Compsons outside historical time, or rather in a time flux, thereby providing Faulkner with the omniscience (and logic) to cover the total range of the novel's action past, present, and future. Given Benjy's basic weakness of mind and his absolute lack of a time sense, dislocations of the time sequences in his section are understandable. Benjy, moreover, is virtually living in that timeless state that Quentin tries so hard to reach.

QUENTIN, OBSESSED WITH TIME. The conscientious reader can find literally hundreds of allusions and/or symbols relating to time in the Quentin section. More than anything else, Quentin would like to get *outside* of time, as Benjy has just about done. There is the classic (or literary) temporary escape — sleep; there is the permanent escape — death. Quentin considers these and several other forms of escape as well. He wants to escape time because he does not wish to give up the intense pain (and the guilt) that Caddy's dishonor has given him. He also wants to escape time because, paradoxically, he has decided (says Perrin Lowrey) "that one way to get outside of time is to kill himself, and he has set a time for his suicide. But if he can manage in some way to *forget* time before the appointed hour, everything will be all right. . . . This is the reason for Quentin's struggle, throughout his section, against finding out what time it is."

Throughout that fateful day of June 2, 1910, Quentin tries various subterfuges to evade or forget time. He purposely breaks his watch, but the watch keeps on ticking; time keeps on going, giving him no escape from *timeness*, or that temporary reprieve from the self-determined death that he is so desperately trying to stretch out. He enters a jeweler's shop, presumably to have the watch fixed, but refuses to leave the watch for repair. Instead, he asks the jeweler if "any of those watches in the window are right?" The jeweler gives him a reassuring answer: none of the watches is correct. Now Quentin knows that watches can lie, that they can measure only *apparent*, not *real*, time (cf. Sartre above). Perhaps he may yet get into real time without killing himself. He will try harder to block out mechanical time from his consciousness simply by avoiding clocks, calendars, and the like. He will have a more diffiult task trying to block out the more natural time-measurer, the sun.

Quentin's dilemma arises from his desire to get out of *temporal* (that is, natural and mechanical) time and into *eternal* or *infinite* time in which change and motion are suspended or transcended and everything remains in the present (Benjy's state, that is) ; but he is not willing to pay the price (at least not yet) — death. He keeps thinking of himself as already dead, or that he will soon be dead. He has eliminated the future in his personal continuum of time; he now tries to disguise (he cannot completely eradicate) the present by using verbs in the past tense or by changing present tenses into past tenses. Thus, the Cartesian "Cogito, ergo *sum*" ("I think, therefore I *am*") would become "Cogito, ergo *eram*" ("I think, therefore I *was*"). As in the case of Benjy's concept (used broadly, of course) of time, Quentin's near-insane obsession with time provides Faulkner with the device for commuting between the past and the present, between the years 1899 and 1910, with a great deal of artistic logic.

FOR JASON, TIME IS MONEY. Jason is also obsessed with time, but in a much different manner and for altogether different motives. However much he may rush from place to place to save time, he never quite gets where he wants to get to in time to accomplish any of his desires. Time, like money, seems to elude him. He "just misses" catching his niece who has absconded with his money (time in this instance would literally be money) ; he gets to the cotton market just too late to save his investment; he continually complains about the lateness with which the cotton market reports come down from New York. "Though he attempts to steal and hoard time just as he does money," Lowrey observes, ". . . his lateness is always self-induced; it is always a product of his almost frantic dashing about. Like a good many of Jason's doings, this tendency to be so busy saving time as never to have any becomes funny." The point Faulkner is making through Jason's misunderstanding of the nature of time is that modern society rejected *real* time when it decided to reject the past, and that its prodigal waste of time (that is, the present) through a mechanical, minute-to-minute measurement of time is a prime example of reason applied without the tempering influence of sensation or emotion. In Jason, therefore, we have the prime example of the modern person who does not understand that time follows "the order of the heart."

DILSEY'S KITCHEN CLOCK. Dilsey is neither obsessed with time, as Quentin and Jason are, nor insensible to it, as Benjy is. For her, time is something concrete, something to be used (but not desperately, as Jason uses it), and also something abstract or eternal (as Quentin sees it). And because she has grasped the true meaning of time, she can function in any crisis, get things done, and even get to church on time to hear about resurrection, the timelessness of faith, eternal life, eternal time. Because of her, the reader is able, for the first time, to see the whole Compson family in "proper historical perspective," which only a correct time-sense, a proper understanding of the continuum of time, can give.

CHRISTIAN PARALLELS. The reader will recall that in answer to a question concerning symbolic meaning of dates in *The Sound and The Fury*, Faulkner said, "it was quite instinctive that I picked out Easter, that I wasn't writing any symbolism of the Passion Week at all." Be that as it may, there is much internal evidence to indicate that Faulkner's instinct, like the guess of a skilled scientist, was an *educated* one. Brought up in a Southern Fundamentalist milieu, exposed for many years to the Bible and to evangelical religion, and totally respectful of past traditions, Faulkner used the Easter week-end of 1928 *with artistic intention* and with extraordinary skill to suggest a set of traditional values in ironic contradistinction to actual values held by many members of the Compson household.

For Quentin, Jason, and Mrs. Compson, traditional Christian rhetoric and theology assume new and perverted meanings as they are used for self-serving ends. For them it is a Calvinism turned morbid — almost tantamout to a "pessimistic naturalism" or "cosmic pessimism" except that "doom" is defined not as the product of natural causes (that is, blind fatalism) but as the will of a very jealous, merciless Old Testament God.

For Dilsey, however, these perverted traditional Christian concepts take on dramatic power through her more mature (albeit more "primitive") Christian faith. She agrees with the Compson (and other) Calvinists that nature and society are "fallen" worlds breeding death, imperfection, and sin. But she parts company with them in respect to *her* concept of God. Because her faith is so much stronger, hers is a personal God rather than an inscrutable, avenging one; her God possesses a divine love that passeth human understanding. Witness, for example, how the Negro preacher's sermon, without denying the natural limits and finite suffering of man (see section above, "To Suffer is to Endure"), suggests that, "like Christ's crucifixion, such experience has meaning beyond a self-pitying awareness of natural death." In the preacher's words, "de resurrection en de light" rather than "de darkness en de death" is the true, life-supporting vision. Dilsey, in her sincere humility ("earthiness"? cf. *The Bear* and the pageant-rite as a prototype of Easter, an "earth celebration" in pagan times), with Benjy (innocence personified) at her side in church, becomes a symbol of individual dignity, endurance, and the possibility of human freedom from all sorts of darkness.

"PASSION PLAY" OF THE COMPSONS. Three of the four sections of *The Sound and The Fury* are set on Easter Sunday and two days preceding it (the dates also serving as section headings). The date of Quentin's monologue falls out on a Thursday (June 2) in 1910 to form a complete, four-part Easter ceremony and celebration from Thursday to Sunday. In Quentin's monologue (says Carvel Collins) may be found several elements of Christ's experience on Holy Thursday; for example: Quentin's "Last Supper" when he joins Shreve and Gerald and their friends in the picnic with its wine ("blood") ; when he "breaks bread" ("body") with the little Italian girl, the act parallels the establishment of the Eucharist and its later ritual, including the pre-sanctification of the Host that takes place on Holy Thursday; in Quentin's tortured conversation with his father, also on Holy Thursday, and paralleling Christ's anguished calling upon *His* Father; finally, Quentin's capture by a mob, as Christ was, and likewise being taken before a magistrate or "high priest."

Jason's section, dated Good Friday, 1928, parallels Christ's experience on the Friday of *His* Passion: the mother of Jesus agonizes with him, and Mrs. Compson appears at some length in this monologue; also Magdalen, in the form of Jason's "girl friend" from Memphis; Jason's name is not only the name of the seeker of the Golden Fleece (as Jason Compson indubitably was), but was also used for "Jesus" by Hellenized Jews; Jesus is placed upon the Cross at Calvary at noon of Good Friday, and dies there *at three o'clock,* and Jason Compson is "commercially crucified" when he begins his speculation in the cotton market at noon and is sold out of the market by his Jewish brokers *at three o'clock.* Finally, after three o'clock, the soul of Christ crucified goes to "harrow Hell"; Jason tells Miss Quentin to go to Hell (she says she will), and after his "commercial crucifixion" is ended, he leaves town to pursue her (with his money) and her carnival friend whose red necktie Jason promises to make "Hell's latchstring."

BENJY-CHRIST IN HELL. Benjy's monologue is dated Holy Saturday, 1928. According to Christian theology, Christ spent Holy Saturday in Hell redeeming such pre-Christian worthies as Father Adam. Benjy likewise emulates Christ's experiences: his birthday candles suggest the paschal candle which figures prominently in church ritual on Holy Saturday; fire fascinates Benjy (it is one of the few things that can keep him quiet) on a day dedicated to the ritualistic lighting of the new fire or "light" (his caretaker-companion at this time is Dilsey's son, Luster, meaning "shine" or light"); Holy Saturday is a traditional day of christening and much goes on on that day about the changing of the idiot's name from Maury to Benjamin.

MISS QUENTIN AND THE "EMPTY TOMB." Events involving the Compson family on Easter Sunday, 1928, parallel those involving Jesus on that day: Miss Quentin's empty room and discarded underthings may symbolize Christ's empty tomb and the discarded shroud.

COMPSONS AND THE ELEVENTH COMMANDMENT. "Examination of these motifs in *The Sound and The Fury*," Carvel Collins concludes, ". . . makes clear that the Compson sons are in parallel with Christ, but, significantly, by inversion. . . . In short, God's Son passed through the events of the Passion and rose as a redeemer; the Compson sons pass through parallel events but go down in failure." And they do so because love, the *eleventh* commandment according to Jesus, was either completely missing or violently distorted in the Compson family.

FROM CHRISTIAN TO FREUDIAN TRINITY. "One problem of part of the novel's Christian parallel is that all three Compson sons appear in parallel with Jesus," Collins suggests, "when a single figure running through the whole parallel would have made for a more easily apprehended unity." Here Collins strains too hard to arrive at a "trinity" or triune form of a Christian God, and, ironically, has to resort to non-Christian and probably atheistic Freud to achieve it. Nonetheless, he says: "But it seems to me that the three Compsons merge at a symbolic level into what is, in a sense, a single figure: Benjamin lives and operates at the level of the primitive and inarticulate id as Freud described it; Quentin at that of the ego, which Freud presented as a battleground between the urges of the id and the restraints of the super-ego; and Jason at that of the repressive super-ego." (Carrying Freud one step farther, one should point out that Jason sublimates his own libido — most of the time — by substituting money for sex.)

On the superficial level, the novel presents three Southern males, three highly individualistic brothers, involved in very credible, concrete events. On a more abstract level, the three brothers may be said to be merged into one personality — if one accepts Freudian theory, as Collins does. "For example," Collins explains, "Benjamin (who, like the id as Freud described it, has no sense whatever of time or sequence) goes to sleep at the end of his monologue; on the next page, in the first sentence of the next son's monologue, Quentin wakes saying (in keeping with Freud's description of the ego as the first part of the personality to become aware of time), 'Then I was in time again.' "

Neither Collins nor anyone else can accurately say whether Faulkner consciously intended applying the Freudian parallel to the story of The Brothers Compson (we shall presently consider what Faulkner *did* say about Collins's Freudian interpretation). Collins would like to believe that Faulkner did so, "for to merge the three sons into one in this way helps not only to pull together the parallel with Christ but to elucidate further the theme of the effect of lack of love."

(For Collins, it is once more back to Christian Fundamentalism!)

When Faulkner was asked where he had learned psychology, he said he didn't know. "Only what I have learned about it from listening to people that do know. What little of psychology I know the characters I have invented and playing poker have taught me. *Freud I'm not familiar with.*" (Italics added) On another occasion, he said (and we quote again), "the writer don't have to know Freud to have written things which anyone who does know Freud can divine and reduce into symbols. And so when the critic finds these symbols, they are of course there. But they were there as inevitably as the critic should stumble on his own knowledge of Freud to discern symbol [sic] ..."

*THE SOUND AND THE FURY* AS FILM. By 1959, when *The Sound and The Fury* was released as a film, Hollywood had already converted to celluloid immortality the following Faulkner works: *Sanctuary* (released under the less enigmatic title of *The Story of Temple Drake*), *Turnabout* (a short story about the war), *Intruder in the Dust*, and *The Hamlet* (combined with the short story, "Barn Burner," and released under the less literary title of *The Long Hot Summer*). Now it was time to put Faulkner's most difficult work on the screen, for, as the producer, Jerry Wald, put it, "Although good films have sometimes been based on second-rate literary sources, the richness and depth of an excellent book cannot help but 'rub off,' as it were, in its transferal to the screen."

Writing of the screen play of *The Sound and The Fury* was entrusted to Irving Ravetch and Harriet Frank, Jr., husband-and-wife team that had done the screenplay *The Long Hot Summer*. The director once again was Martin Ritt. In doing the former screenplay, the Ravetches did not attempt to follow the plot or even use all the characters of *The Hamlet*; they were interested mainly in getting into their screenplay "the flavor and spirit of an aspect of Faulkner's work" — the broad, salty, grassroots kind of humor. For the screenplay of *The Sound and The Fury*, the writers found their clue in a statement made by Faulkner himself in the *Paris Review* interview, to wit, that the story "is set in motion by a young girl in a Mississippi family, without love or affection or understanding, who climbs down a rainpipe to flee from the only home she ever knew." So, for Hollywood, the story of Miss Quentin, as unfolded in the fourth section mainly, would become the focus of the screenplay. This episode, according to the producer, "is most clearly related in the novel in its fourth, objectively recounted section," and it would thus seem most expedient to skip the first three complicated sections of the novel (he did promise that although we do not hear Benjy's disconnected thoughts in the film, some of the data provided in that first section have "been worked into the warp and woof of our drama") and begin with the objective narrative and gradually unfold the weight of the past through this. (One must bear in mind that Hollywood had laid claim to the flashback long before Faulkner did, and would thus have no difficulty jumping from the fourth section to the first — or second or third — section of the novel.)

"Adaptation" implies "interpretation," and in film-making there is great latitude for the collaborative team (writers, director, cameramen, editors, producer, *et al*). Changes are made even as the team recognizes that "we may not have produced a film that will not wholly please those purists who find any sort of 'tampering' with a literary 'masterpiece' a kind of sacrilege." And since the film must appeal to a larger audience than that for the book, in the process of transference to the screen the work will lose some of the flavor and subtlety of the original form. "Therefore," wrote Hollis Alpert in reviewing the film in *The Saturday Review* of March 7, 1959, "Faulkner's original hangs over the movie only in ghostly fashion." Several changes were suggested by the "interpreters" themselves; others arose from using as the major source of background material the Appendix that Faulkner himself wrote for the Viking Portable edition of his works (to be discussed at the end of this chapter). The "team" did not make a "travesty" out of the book, says Alpert, but "something that is very good on its level. They have taken suggestions for a story by Faulkner, and then gone ahead to create their own Compson family."

Miss Quentin occupies the largest part of the story in the film, thereby enhancing the roles of Caddy and Jason through her relations with them. It also helps when the actress available for the part is Joanne Woodward, who gives a remarkably convincing performance as the moody, rebellious, Southern teenager at odds with a dying family, an absentee mother, and a rapacious uncle. The viewer is not at all shocked, therefore, when she seems ready to run off with the first lusty stranger (red tie or not) to make a pass at her. The role of Caddy is played by Margaret Leighton, who much later in her theatrical and movie career picked up the more genuine Southern glamor and flavor through performing in works by Tennessee Williams. In this film, she is a bit too restrained (she is Candace rather than Caddy), especially in the scene where she meets the seventeen-year-old daughter she abandoned at birth. *This* Caddy definitely belongs to the Appendix rather than to the book proper.

But it is in the characters of Jason and Quentin that the film gives the purists most reason to writhe. For Jason, the producer had available the actor, Yul Brynner, with the right temperament for the part but with an unmistakably *un*Southern accent. The accent was made acceptable "by changing the nationality of Jason and his aging mother to French — from the Bayou country in Louisiana." How Faulkner's Caroline Compson would have loved that! Moreover, a Jason born in Louisiana rather than in Mississippi must now be endowed with finer motivations for his actions than those mentioned in the novel. "In the process of dramatization this *positive* note seemed essential," the producer said. Why essential? But since the rest of the characters are left "virtually intact" (there is more than a slight demurrer to be entered on behalf of Quentin's revised role), the producer trusts that "this one change has not prevented us from rendering the tone and quality of Faulkner's book."

What to do with Quentin? He committed suicide eighteen years before the date of the other three sections. There is no "follow-up" for him in the Appendix to the novel. Why not pretend he never did get around to taking his own life and that he is still around in the film "as he would surely have become if he had failed in his attempt to take his life: an aging, gentle alcoholic living dimly in his memory of the past." We are grateful to the producer for that "extension" of Faulkner's Quentin. It is very possible, however, that the writers may have had in mind the character of Quentin's father, and may have expanded Quentin's heavy reliance on his father into a total assumption of the father's character by Quentin.

One final note on character transformation as it takes place from novel to film. In the film there is a very close, warm relationship between Jason and Miss Quentin. The reader naturally presumes that she is his niece. In the novel, yes; in the film, no. (In 1959, films rarely if ever touched upon incest.) Miss Quentin may be attracted to the carnival man for a time, but she is soon back to the more familiar arms of Jason. The film strongly implies, moreover, that she will marry Jason. (Jason, the greatest of Faulkner's villains, now a romantic, middle-aged man for whom a passionate teenager can fall!)

"I am often asked what Mr. Faulkner thinks about all this," the producer of *The Sound and The Fury* observed in an article entitled "From Faulkner to Film," in *The Saturday Review* of March 7, 1959. In selling the film rights to *any* of his books, Faulkner put no restrictions on the purchaser except that he, Faulkner, would not be required to read the script or see the film. And in the case of this book, completed thirty years before the film, it probably cannot change what has been done. "I only hope that, if by any chance Mr. Faulkner *does* wander into his local theatre in Oxford, Mississippi, while *The Sound and The Fury* is playing, he will recognize the good faith of our effort." The record does not show that Faulkner ever helped the producer realize that fond hope.

But let's not be snobbish about the matter of novels converted into films. Faulkner himself did quite a bit of "adapting" or "editing" of "masterpieces" by other writers, and presumably took equally great liberties with their works. One can name Raymond Chandler's *The Big Sleep* and Ernest Hemingway's *To Have and Have Not,* two examples that immediately come to mind. Then there was the "tampering" that he did with his own *Sanctuary, Intruder in the Dust,* and several short stories.

The fact is that Jerry Wald, in producing *The Sound and The Fury,* was trying to create a kind of hybrid film made up of part Faulkner and part Hollywood ("with a dash of Actor's Studio and some Tennessee Williams flavoring tossed in," Hollis Alpert adds). "The mixture," Alpert concludes, "is not unpalatable." Alpert found this Faulkner film better than *The Long Hot Summer* (formerly *The Hamlet*), and probably more acceptable if it had come before *A Streetcar Named Desire, Baby Doll,* and *The Long Hot Summer.* "But the failure who drinks away his love for his sister, the mother who becomes a tramp rather than look after her daughter, the girl groping for her identity —" all this we have heard before, says Alpert. "The details are fine, but the message we have had before," and in less ponderous — or pompous — a treatment.

APPENDIX TO *THE SOUND AND THE FURY.* Fifteen years after publication (and sixteen years after the writing) of *The Sound and The Fury,* Faulkner was reminded that his favorite book, the one he called "the most gallant, the most magnificent failure," was never really completed. When

Malcolm Cowley asked him to write a preface or explanatory note to the book for *The Portable Faulkner* that he was to edit, Faulkner wrote an Appendix which included a genealogy of the Compson family, a detailed map of Yoknapatawpha County, and an account of what happened to the surviving Compsons after 1928. "It was the one that I anguished the most over," Faulkner said of *The Sound and The Fury*, "that I worked the hardest at, that even when I knew I couldn't bring it off, I still worked at it."

And he must have worked at it in a most conscientious manner, for after one reads the Appendix with its elaborate Compson genealogy and other features (and this written sixteen years after the publication of the novel, and, according to Cowley, without a single copy of the novel before him), the whole novel falls into a definite pattern "like a jigsaw puzzle when the magician's wand touched it." The Appendix is in no sense a sequel to the novel, although the reader's appetite is whetted to find out more about Benjy (he is committed to an institution in 1933), about Caddy and her Nazi husband, and about Jason and his new career as a Southern tycoon now qualified to compete in the same league with the up-and-coming Snopeses. We shall draw upon some of this "new" material in our next section.

# CHARACTERIZATION IN
## *THE SOUND AND THE FURY*

Before we analyze Faulkner's characters, a word on the Compsons as a family and as individuals may be in order. Cleanth Brooks has observed that "The downfall of the house of Compson is the kind of degeneration which can occur, and has occurred, anywhere at any time. The real significance of the Southern setting in *The Sound and The Fury* resides, as so often elsewhere in Faulkner, in the fact that the breakdown of a family can be exhibited more poignantly and significantly in a society which is old-fashioned and in which the family is still at the center."

The family as an institution began to break up long before Faulkner (or any other Southerner) started taking notice of that sociological phenomenon. Dissolution of the institution may have gone even further in the more sophisticated suburban areas — North, East, and West — than in the small towns in the South, and with much less notice taken of the fact. "For that very reason," Brooks concludes, "what happens to the Compsons might make less noise and cause less comment, and even bring less pain to the individuals concerned, if the Compsons lived in a more progressive and liberal environment." More progressive, and probably more liberated from such old-fashioned ideals and traditions as "close family loyalty, home care for defective children, and the virginity of unmarried daughters."

BENJY AS PROLOGUE. "He was a prologue," said Faulkner, "like the gravedigger in the Elizabethan dramas. He serves his purpose and is gone. Benjy is incapable of good and evil because he had no knowledge of good and evil." Benjy wasn't selfish either; he lacked the rational capacity to be so. He was almost pure "animal," with a mind that worked, not by association which relies to some extent on such skills as discrimination and comparison, but by a kind of mechanical identification. This mechanical identification is further illustrated, says Olga Vickery, "by his inflexible identification of one word with one object. Very seldom, for example, is the name of a speaker replaced by a pronoun in his section."

Benjy does have the capacity to recognize tenderness and love, however, though he would probably be incapable of naming them. It was unquestionably the threat to tenderness and love that moved him to bellow when he *felt* the change in Caddy. Caddy was gone; but, being an idiot, he could not be aware of her absence. He knew (in his own way) only that *something* was wrong, was missing, and it was that vacuum which he tried to fill.

Within this rigid world, Benjy both orders and evaluates his experience; objects he has learned to recognize (or sense) represent an inflexible pattern which he struggles to defend against any change, a struggle that is signaled by every bellow in his oversized body. "Within this rigid world," Vickery observes, "Caddy is at once the focus of order and the instrument of its destruction." Benjy loves her as much as he loves the *pasture*, the *fire*, and *sleep*, three things (plus, of course, the smell of trees) he associates with her.

After Caddy leaves, the only reminder he has of her is one of her discarded slippers. "The slipper was his tenderness and love," Faulkner said, adding that "The slipper gave him comfort even though he no longer remembered the person to whom it had belonged, any more than he could remember why he grieved. If Caddy had reappeared he probably would not have known her." Cleanth Brooks adds that "Benjy represents love in its most simple and childlike form. His love for Caddy is intense and unreflective."

**BENJY AS BEAUTIFUL, HELPLESS ANGEL.** "Benjy is beautiful, as beautiful as one of the helpless angels," says Evelyn Scott, "and the more so for the slightly repellent earthiness that is his." Nor does this angel-idiot, endowed with this earthiness, have to go much farther to suggest the "animal" that Faulkner speaks of. "It is as if, indeed, Blake's Tiger had been framed before us by the same Hand that made the Lamb," Scott suggests, "and, in opposition to Blake's conception, endowed with the same soul. Innocence is terrible as well as pathetic — and Benjy is terrible, sometimes terrifying."

**BENJY AND LOSS OF LOVE.** Benjy as "prologue" enunciates the main theme of the novel — the loss of love is the actual cause of decay in modern society. "All the other aspects of deterioration, social and moral, apparent in the juxtaposition of Benjy's childhood world and his adult life, are symptomatic," says Edmund Volpe. By the time he reaches the age of thirty-three, Benjy has lost many things; but in his loss of Caddy he has lost the most precious thing of all — love. His present is a remembrance of things *lost* — the Compson pasture (Benjy's pasture) now a golf course, the "graveyard" (two stalks of jimson weeds in a bottle), the fire, Caddy's white satin slipper — all memorializing, like gravestones, so many precious things lost.

The function of Section I (of Benjy, to be sure) is to permit the past to expose the sterility of the present, and the most strongly symbolic component of the past is childhood — Benjy's childhood. The Compson family may be falling apart socially, economically, and morally, but this is of little concern to Benjy who can neither perceive nor comprehend the process of decay (One is reminded of a line from the Latin poet Catullus: "Nescio, et excrucior" "I don't know why, but I am tormented nonetheless"). Benjy suffers from the loss of Caddy, the "emotional center for his childhood world," Volpe calls it.

BENJY AND ILLUSION OF HAPPINESS RESTORED. For a brief moment (in Section IV) Benjy imagines he has regained the happiness he lost with the loss of Caddy. In the closing scene, the irresponsible Luster has taken Benjy for a ride in the carriage and has just driven the carriage to the left (or wrong) side of the statue of the Confederate soldier standing in the square. Benjy's conditioned reaction to this departure from common routine is an agonized bellow. Jason ("the villainous representation of the corruption in the new South") seizes the reins from Luster ("indolent, careless, traditional") and sets the customary pattern aright by violence. Faulkner describes Benjy's eyes now as "empty and blue and serene again as cornice and facade flowed smoothly once more from left to right; post and tree, window and doorway, and signboard, each in its ordered place." Jason's violent, direct action restores Benjy's illusioned happiness, but only for the moment; Jason has also broken the stem of the single flower that Benjy has been holding in his hand. The symbolism is obvious: Jason is ashamed of his brother and would love to have him (the past, the Compson past, the Southern past) out of the way. In the Appendix to the novel, we learn that Jason does just that in 1933, when he has Benjy committed to the institution at Jackson (by this time both Mrs. Compson and Dilsey, the two strongest dissenters, have gone).

QUENTIN: NURSING AN OBSESSION. The Benjy section presented a picture of disintegration in one specific family, but with implications for a much larger segment of the "human family" today. Paradoxically, this largeness of reference came through even though it was a tale *about* and *told by* an idiot. (Reference was made earlier to the original meaning of the  Greek word *idiotes*, or "individual.") The reason may be that Benjy the idiot is symbolic of the *whole* Compson clan from way back, to a time of original innocence when they were close to the soil and nature, before they were corrupted and confused by the abandonment of nature (cf. *The Bear*) in favor of the materialism of society.

The Quentin section immediately reduces the scope of the novel to a problem *of an individual,* a problem (as we shall show below) that carries with it implications to gladden the heart of almost every amateur (and professional) psychologist and psychiatrist. The problem at times even separates itself from the Compson history proper. "Where Benjy recalls a world," Howe observes, "Quentin nurses an obsession." Is it also possible that Quentin is (in the stricter sense of the word) the "idiot"?

Quentin does try hard to rise above being merely a psychological case and to become part of, and to define, the complete nature and significance of the Compson tragedy. He fails, however, because of his obsession combined with his innate weakness, passivity, and general confusion. "Benjy, though an idiot, reveals the family situation more faithfully than Quentin," Howe maintains, "for the events Benjy remembers tell us more than the efforts of Quentin to comprehend them."

QUENTIN'S WORLD. Quentin's world is a bifurcated one. On that fateful day (June 2, 1910), he shuttles back and forth between two sets of events, one past and the other present. On one plane, he can function quite normally (or mechanically) with common personal chores; on another plane, his mind is fitfully occupied with echoes of the ever-intrusive past almost to the detriment of the performance of those necessary, pedestrian tasks before the close of the day (and his life). Quentin's problem arises from his inability to separate his memories of the past from his involvement with the present.

Quentin's world is thus perforce made up of a melange of symbols and recurrent phrases that constantly clash with the more palpable evidences of the present. Historical and literary allusions — Jesus, St. Francis, Moses, Washington, Byron, and even Benjy as "Benjamin the child of mine old age held hostage into Egypt" and Caddy as "Eve or Little Sister Death" — serve to diminish the "realness" of the reality in which he must function, and of the nature against which he is constantly struggling. Fragrance of honeysuckle chokes him, but this is no mere allergy. Honeysuckle represents for Quentin "the ripe animality of sex, the incomprehensible and hateful world for which Caddy has abandoned his paradise, and hence it is also the symbol of his defeat." In Quentin's world, honeysuckle cannot be a mere sensation, nor can Caddy's affair with Dalton Ames be construed merely as a natural event.

QUENTIN: REFLECTIONS IN A GLASS. Quentin's flight from reality and substance is further emphasized by references to shadows and mirrors. True, Benjy also sees Caddy's wedding reflected in a mirror; but when Quentin sees the reflection, it is as if Caddy runs out of the mirror and out of his world; Quentin has "canceled" her out of reality. He also cancels her out of his own private world by seeing her (and Dalton Ames) in silhouette or in shadow. Since he cannot accept the "natural" facts of her love affair and her marriage, which he finds "perverse, mocking, denying the significance they should have confirmed," he denies them substance, and so ostracizes them from his own world.

QUENTIN, WHOSE NAME WAS "WRIT IN WATER." When shadow images begin to fuse with water images (and one should bear in mind that the *water surface* itself is still another kind of mirror), the reader may conclude that death by water will be Quentin's way of bringing his two worlds together, of fusing shadow and reality, thus minimizing the antagonism between them. "Whatever suggestion of purification may be present, water is primarily a symbol of oblivion for Quentin," Olga Vickery says. Like Keats, Quentin's name is to be "writ in water." Both Caddy and Quentin keep running to the Branch (brook) to lose themselves in an unconsciousness (paradise?) brought on by the water's hypnotic rhythm, and surrendering themselves to the blurring effect of the water on thought, emotion, and the necessity for action (innocence?). It is as if they were seeking out

that "Garden of Eden" in which they could be both sister
and brother *and* husband and wife *in all innocence* (of incest,
for one) ; or that they were seeking out the peace and innocence in the amniotic fluid of the universal womb.

QUENTIN: ETHICS IN STASIS. Quentin possesses an
ethical system based on words, on "fine, dead sound," devoid
of all real meaning because the system was arrived at *a
priori*, before experience. Nor will he agree to subject this
system to experience to ascertain its true meaning and value.
He chooses to separate ethics from the total context of human
action and behavior. Quentin is both shocked and confused
when his concept of virginity, for example, comes into conflict with Caddy's loss of virginity in the context of experience. Moreover, since Quentin is all thought and little
or no emotion, he is incapable of loving anybody, even Caddy.
In short, "Despite his feverish preoccupation with ethics,"
says Vickery, "he is unable to perform any ethical actions
himself; even his death is not so much a protest as it is simply
a withdrawal."

Quentin's ethics at times seem to attempt to break out of
their static form in a rather perverse way. For example,
does he see incest (with Caddy) as preferable to and even
more noble than the surrender of a woman's virginity to a
stranger? His reference to Benjy and Egypt (Biblically he
is in error, of course) calls to mind the attitude toward incest
within the royal family of Egypt, where it was condoned.
Did Adam and Eve, (Quentin calls Caddy "Eve" and "Little
Sister Death") then, commit the *first* act of incest? There is
also the matter of Quentin's Puritanism. He is one of Faulkner's most assertive Puritans, and his Puritanism comes out
most noticeably in his alarm at the breakdown of sexual
morality. When the standards of sexual morality are threatened, "a common reaction and one quite natural to Puritanism," Cleanth Brooks points out, "is to try to define some
point beyond which surely no one would venture to transgress
— to find at least one act so horrible that everyone would be

repelled by it." To Quentin, that one horrible act would probably be Caddy's fall from chastity, and not incest. *"I have committed incest I said Father it was I it was not Dalton Ames,"* Quentin says (pp. 97-98). And Quentin recalls his father saying ". . . and now this other you are not lying now either but you are still blind to what is in yourself to that part of general truth the sequence of natural events and their causes which shadows every mans brow even benjys . . ." (p. 220). But Quentin cannot agree.

QUENTIN AS ROMANTIC. Another way of looking at Quentin is to compare him with the Eternal Romantic, the literary stereotype of the egocentric, narcissistic individual holding on to an impossible ideal (dream, shadow, memory) in the face of hard reality. Quentin is Hamlet — melancholy, indecisive, and misanthropic — a man out of season. Quentin is Macbeth — cynical about life in general ("life's but a walking shadow"). Quentin is Dostoyevsky's Raskolnikov — concerned about his sister's virginity, dividing most of his university time between ineffectual study and the contemplation of murder or suicide by drowning. Quentin resembles James Joyce's Stephen Dedalus — full of guilt, preoccupied with time, alienated (against his will) from family and homeland. Quentin may be, most of all, T. S. Eliot's J. Alfred Prufrock — weak, spiritless, life-fearing, "Do I dare?" Or, Quentin is *all of these*, "trying to live in a private inner world of their own," says Robert Slabey, "in a way committing intellectual incest."

Quentin is also the greatest of all lovers — the lover denied love. Knowing that he cannot find real love in life, he seeks out death, even as he waits for some more earthly answer to his quest. But because he lives in a world of concepts rather than actions, he strenuously shies away from real experience with love. Reason must transcend passion, the ideal must take precedence over the real. Some romantics are in love with love; Quentin is in love with death.

QUENTIN AND "LITTLE SISTER EVE." Quentin's private inner world was shattered when Caddy lost her virginity. Quentin's cosy world of childhood idealism and fantasy — and innocence — was attacked when Caddy violated the traditional social and religious codes of the Compsons and the whole South (as Quentin knew, or imagined, it to be). But why his reaction to this assault on the concept of female purity should have been so positive, so violent, so conducive to the making of a commitment to suicide, is hardly to be explained by righteous indignation or by a feeling of complicity in a mortal attack on the very bastions of Southern morality. The answer lies more probably in his repressed desire to cohabit with his sister, or with his mother through Caddy, the mother-substitute. Quentin says: *"If I'd just had a mother so I could say Mother, Mother"* (p. 190). Mrs. Compson, *as a mother*, just wasn't there. But Caddy was, until . . .

Until Caddy announced that she was to marry Herbert Head, Quentin still felt that Caddy was with him. Caddy's loss of honor was actually not as serious a blow to him as the loss of Caddy herself. With her marriage, their "blissful" relationship would be terminated, and he would then seriously begin considering suicide (p. 152). Quentin's emotional and physical dependence on Caddy is so great that he translates all his idealism into terms of her conduct. Religious and moral values translate into her sexual innocence; all those values prevailed so long as they were both children and innocent. Caddy was his "little sister Eve." For both Benjy and Quentin, reality crashed into a dream world of innocence when little sister Caddy grew up and became a non-virgin (p. 172). Incest, too, symbolized the intrusion of reality upon his "pure" relationship with Caddy. Why does Quentin want to *say* that he committed incest rather than *do* it? Was this his idea of *clean* sex? Was the repressed desire less of a sin? "His sole desire," Volpe concludes, "is to isolate himself and Caddy somehow from the rest of the world as they were isolated during their childhood." Like Adam and Eve *before* the fall?

QUENTIN AS ETERNAL ADOLESCENT. An eminent sociologist has described the present state of American society as a product of "built-in adolescence." Of course, a generalization is never the sum total of all the particular cases examined. Quentin, like so many other men both in the South and the North, suffered (according to Volpe) from "an adolescent mind in stasis." That is, his mind refused to let go of most (or at least some) of the idealized childhood vision in the face of an increased awareness of the new reality around him. Quentin held on to the past as if it were a security blanket, a favorite toy, his first teddy bear. His "toy," however, was a very big one, merely the *whole* tradition of plantation aristocracy in its most refined — and romanticized — form. Quentin saw himself as the self-appointed custodian of a tradition which encompassed gentility, chivalry, and all the other accepted and practiced virtues. (In this respect, he very closely resembles Faulkner himself.) Quentin remembered the Negroes of his childhood with much affection (as did Faulkner; we shall soon touch upon this matter in greater detail), and in the Blands of Cambridge he recognized a scaled-down, deteriorated version of social customs of that same long-lost plantation society.

Quentin's emotional difficulties (the psychologist would call them "disturbances") compel him to defy reality, time, and his own physical and intellectual development (Harvard doesn't help him much in this respect) by remaining a child. (Through suicide, he remains a child, albeit a dead one.) He longs for the sexlessness of childhood (this point was covered earlier in some detail), and tries to ignore the fact of adult sex. "If adult sex were completely alien to him, as it is in childhood," Volpe concludes, "then it could not disturb him" (p. 135).

QUENTIN AS HERO. Quentin is no tragic hero; he is too weak, defeatist, too lacking in will to resist any of the pressures of reality in a positive, heroic way; he is pathetic. "What we respond to is, of course," observes John L. Longley, "the sense of tragic waste and loss — the self-inflicted death of so much sensitivity and perception." Quentin is not a mere abstraction, but a real human being and an authentic creature of a specific culture, despite his "anguished speculations upon the nature of time" and his frenetic attempts to take himself "out of time." He is, in Cleanth Brooks's words, "a young man who has received a grievous psychic wound."

JASON'S PETTY WORLD. Faulkner had also called Jason "The first sane Compson since before Culloden . . . ," but Section III of *The Sound and The Fury* presents a picture of the world as seen through a glass made up of the petty, sadistic lunacy of Jason, the last of the Compsons, the son who had to stay home instead of going off to Harvard, the unstable country-store clerk always threatening to leave his miserable position, the failure — up to now. Jason is going mad, and knows it (even if Faulkner doesn't know it, or pretends not to know it). But the madness is less of a mental deterioration than a spiritual one. He is emotionally disposed against reflection and self-examination. His madness is "a bland, immediate state of soul, which he feels encroaching on his meager, objectively considered universe," Evelyn Scott points out. "He is in an agony of inexplicable anticipation of disaster for which his cruelties afford him no relief."

JASON — FACTS, FACTS, FACTS. Jason is objective to a fault. He prides himself on the fact that he has no illusions about the Compsons or about himself. He sees and tells it *like it is* (he thinks). He is convinced that what others may consider a distorted view of Caddy, the other Compsons, and mankind in general, is really an objective conclusion reached by him on the basis of facts alone. Jason is always trying to organize his thoughts, values, and actions in such a way that they will not be threatened by the irrational. "It is his method of assuming control over experience," according to Olga Vickery, "by preventing himself from becoming involved in circumstances he has not foreseen." His efforts, while superficially villainous most of the time, are often comic as well. Jason has no love for Caddy, for any of the other Compsons, for his Memphis "girlfriend," or for any other human being. "The relationship he desires is a commercial one: you know where you stand; there is no romantic nonsense about it," says Brooks. "Jason, if he could, would reduce all relationships to commercial transactions."

JASON AS CONSUMMATE BUSINESSMAN. Jason is the typical, shabby small-town businessman, narrow in point of view and imagination, grubby in his attitude toward the finer values, and impatient of people who let personal feelings get in the way of business transactions. Jason is not necessarily a dishonest businessman, but he is a villain, a Faulkner villain, a man who lacks the capacity for love. This incapacity reveals itself in two ways (in essence, one way): the attitudes toward nature and women. Jason obviously has no interest in nature (in land, as a negotiable commodity, yes; in land as a natural resource, no); his interest in women, except as objects to be manipulated (his mother, Caddy, Miss Quentin), is almost non-existent. Jason is an almost-virgin, substituting money for sex. We read nothing substantial about his sex life until after 1933 (see Appendix), when he takes up with his Memphis "girlfriend" on a much more regular basis. He can never live down the one "transaction" in which he was beaten (and that by a woman, no less): Miss Quentin's absconding with all of his money.

JASON AS FUNCTIONING ADULT. Of the three Compson brothers, Benjy never left childhood, Quentin remained trapped in adolescence, and Jason alone achieved adulthood. Was it because he was mentally superior to Benjy (obviously) and emotionally better restrained than Quentin (obviously), or was it because he could recognize in the values of society in his day the same values that he espoused? But this is an ironic adjustment, made at the cost of his alienation from his family and from people he works and trades with. He is sick (and here Volpe agrees with Vickery), and "his irrational acts give the lie to his facade of rationality." Jason is an incipient, nascent Snopes; as one of "them," he can function as an adult while his brothers cannot "because the vision of life that he brings out of his childhood approximates the reality of the world." (See Jason as sadist, below.) Devoid of all normal human feeling, Jason can fit comfortably into modern society. By substituting cruelty and unfeelingness for his father's honest cynicism, Jason emerges as an "adjusted" Mr. Compson.

JASON AND THE COMPSON TRADITION. Now, however, as replacement for Mr. Compson, as surrogate head of the family (especially after 1912, the date of Mr. Compson's death), Jason is also employed by his mother as an ally against the enemy, the whole Compson family. Jason is more of a Bascomb than a Compson, she says, and proceeds to spoil him even as she sets him against his father, brothers, and sister. She feels inferior as an individual even as she feels superior to the Compsons as a Bascomb. The psychological confusion resulting therefrom spurs her on to reshape Jason away from the Compson tradition of gentility, nobility, honor, and the like, so that he becomes an extremely selfish individual capable of hating everybody, especially the Compsons and everything they stood for. Jason scoffs at both family ancestry and family tradition (p. 198). His mother has succeeded in molding him into an exaggerated reflection of herself, "carrying to extremes her self-absorption, her superficial social and moral values, her alienation from people," Volpe points out. "His attachment to her is deep, and though he is frequently rude and unkind, he consistently defers to her wishes." Most important of all, he reinforces her in her illusion of being a "Southern lady."

JASON AS SADIST. If it is normal to be a sadist, then Jason is normal, and Faulkner was correct when he called Jason "the first sane Compson since Culloden" and "rational, contained and even a philosopher in the old stoic tradition." Somehow one gets the feeling that Faulkner is once again playing tricks with the reader (at least in the Appendix), because very early in the novel (p. 79) Faulkner gave us strong intimations of Jason's sadistic streak: "He cut up all the dolls Mau — Benjy and I made," Caddy said. "He did it just for meanness."

There is a little bit of Jason in all of us, and that should disturb us. Jason personifies the instinctive, irrational love of self, the self-concern that often leaves no room for love of others. "Since we dare not admit the fear of imperfection in the self that is loved," John L. Longley observes, "we seek out and punish others in retaliation for any frustration or thwarting that the self encounters." In that respect, Jason is a "normal" sadist.

But Jason carries his "normality" to exceptionally individualistic extremes. If the rest of predictable humanity operates on an emotional basis — pity, generosity, love, pride — he will act otherwise, distrust humanity, and so avoid becoming as weak or as "insane" as they are. But Jason *is* the insane one, captivated by his delusive vision of a humanity whose obligation to respond to *his* needs leaves him no other choice but to blame it for all his frustrations and to punish or torture it for being what it is. He keeps a kind of scoreboard on the number of times he has tortured his mother and Caddy by deceiving them and by lying to each about the other. He enjoys these lies even as he tells them, and enjoys memories of them even more so. For him, lying is a cunning, premeditated process, rather than the feeble human evasion or expedient that it usually is.

Jason is most sadistic, however, in his relationship with his niece, Miss Quentin. In her he sees living proof of Cad-

THE SOUND AND THE FURY

dy's fall from honor; she is also the living reminder of the bank job he did not get when Caddy's first husband learned of the illegitimate child and withdrew his offer of the job. She is, therefore, the proper target for his hatred, cruelty, and retaliation, and he makes the most of this "warrant" for his sadism. At times, Jason's hatred reaches such heights as to force one to conclude that it is a reflection of a deeply repressed incestuous desire for her. (The reader might recall how the film version of the novel actually highlighted this interpretation. Is Hollywood, then, sometimes more perceptive than we give it credit for?)

"The entire pattern of Jason's life, both inward and outward," Longley concludes, "is perfectly adjusted to his needs and desires." (Perhaps Faulkner was confusing the pragmatic with the rational in his evaluation of Jason's sanity.) The whole Compson family and household (which included Dilsey among Jason's "six worthless niggers" to feed) contribute an essential component to the "pattern of self-justification and outraged martyrdom which is Jason's image of himself."

JASON'S "RESURRECTION." The fourth and final section, Easter Sunday, is generally considered to belong to Dilsey. Yet Jason intrudes to such an extent as to make the reader wonder whether Faulkner's not-so-secret admiration for Jason influenced him to give Jason's vigorous pursuit of Miss Quentin and the stolen money so much of the "stage." The contrast is both ironic and artistically necessary (once we analyze it) : to show the tremendous gap between Dilsey's nobility and Jason's meanness, and to show how Jason, as forerunner of the society to come, will "rise" above the temporary defeat inflicted on him by a dying, faith-ridden group of "good" people.

As Longley suggests, "For Jason, as for Quentin, Easter is in a powerfully ironic sense a day of awakening and flight." Quentin has already fled, money, lover, and all, to a future that cannot be (according to Jason) any better or different than her mother's was. For Jason, Easter Sunday will cause him to awaken to a new reality — no more easy money, no more sadistic idleness, no more Quentin to blame for all his frustrations. But for him, "resurrection" has been merely deferred: the Appendix tells us that Jason very soon after is freed of his mother, Benjy, and Dilsey, and launched on a career that is soon (but not too soon) to rival that of the Snopeses. Moreover, with the Compson Mile disposed of (to Flem Snopes as the site of a new airport), Jason now has plenty of money to spend on himself. He makes more money as a cotton buyer, and spends even more on himself. He mellows a bit, now that society has paid its debt to him for all the injustices it had visited upon him. Maybe this is how it should be: if society cannot contain or eliminate such menaces as Jason, then it must find ways in which to tame them. The most common way, it seems, is to "integrate them into the system." Thus integrated, Jason — all the Jasons — becomes "modern man."

JASON AS MODERN MAN. In the final scene, Jason as "modern man" takes over from Luster, "traditional, inefficient man." Jason Compson, like other Faulkner villains (Flem Snopes, Popeye, et al) represents a tragic waste of human resources and feelings; not in themselves but in what they do to others. They are villains because they are dehumanized; because they have chosen to discard most of the traditional human values; because they shun any unprofitable human relationships; and because they consider any show of emotion as a sign of weakness. Significantly enough, Jason (and the others) is a very contemporary figure. He, like all the others in his class, has become what he is (according to Longley) "under the seductions of modern capitalism." "If this is the direction modern man is taking," Longley concludes, "as Faulkner sometimes seems to be saying it is, then perhaps the villains stand for all of us."

"REAL" DILSEY. The Faulkner family's Negro nurse, "Mammy," Callie Barr, remained in William Faulkner's employ until she died in 1940; and in dedicating *Go Down, Moses* (1942) to this woman "who was born in slavery and who gave to my family a fidelity without stint or calculation of recompense and to my childhood an unmeasurable devotion and love," Faulkner was suggesting qualities that appear in the Compsons' servant, Dilsey.

DILSEY, MUTE HISTORIAN OF THE COMPSONS. With the last section, the novel opens up and out from the closed world of the Compsons into the public world as represented by "Greater" Jefferson and Mattson. The Compson Mile is in a state of disintegration and shrinkage. Before the last vestige of it is sold to Flem Snopes for his airport, it will shrink considerably more as the town begins "to encroach and then nibble at and into it." In the Compson house itself, only Dilsey's kitchen, the hearth and heart of the house, shows any semblance of having been lived in; the other rooms are just so many haunted rooms in a decrepit museum. Life and history have deserted the Compsons.

Whatever remains of Compson history may be found in Dilsey's kitchen. "I've seed de first en de last," Dilsey tells Freny. "I seed de beginnin, en now I sees de endin." Quentin left a long time ago. Mr. Compson died two years after Quentin's suicide. Time has virtually erased any memory of Caddy (except for the regular money allowance she sends for Miss Quentin), the one member of the family whose real existence was a product of the minds and memories of those whom she had affected. But Dilsey endures, and because she does, the Compson family acquires some substance and historical value. Without her, the danger is that (according to Vickery) "the sound and the fury of the family signifies very little if anything."

DILSEY AGAINST THE MODERN WORLD. Faulkner has chosen Dilsey not only as his proxy historian of the

Compson family but also as the character through whom he can dramatize positive aspects of his own views about life and society. Dilsey is a "primitive," and as such is far removed from social man. As such, she is also free to rely on faith and hope, far removed from the complex society that produces the Compsons and other hitherto fine families in Faulkner's South destined to be assailed and eventually destroyed by the ruthless wave of commercialism, materialism, and modernism.

Who was Faulkner's choice for the model human being in this novel about "two women"? About Caddy he said that "To me she was the beautiful one, she was my heart's darling. That's what I wrote the book about . . ." He would have preferred Caddy, but his innate Puritanism prevented him from doing so. Instead, he chose Dilsey, and thus renounced, in essence, the modern world with its sexuality and social and economic intercourse. By rejecting Caddy — and Jason — he became, in effect, Quentin. *The Sound and The Fury* may then be described, with some justification, as Faulkner's own *symbolic suicide*.

More and more as the fourth section of the novel develops, Dilsey emerges as a major character and a human being, rather than a mere Negro servant and old faithful retainer. She is there as a yardstick by which deficiencies of the Compsons may be gauged. What is Jason when compared with Dilsey? The two are in constant conflict — first over Caddy and Benjy, then over Miss Quentin — and both prove to be equally strong, strong, that is, in the fact that both survive. "But her endurance," as Vickery sees it, "has strength to suffer without rancor as well as to resist, to accept as well as to protest." Above everything else, however, she poses a challenge to the viability, validity, and efficacy (as well as the desirability) of the kind of world that he would like to live in and for which he seems to be best fitted temperamentally and philosophically. Try as he might, he cannot come up with a force or faith to counter her passive and irrational resistance.

**DILSEY AND UNIVERSAL TRUTHS.** In his Nobel Prize speech, Faulkner spoke of the "old universal truths lacking which any story is ephemeral and doomed — love and honor and pity and pride and compassion and sacrifice. . . ." The statement was a reaffirmation of what he had proclaimed much earlier *through Dilsey* in *The Sound and The Fury*. There is little doubt that Dilsey was intended to represent the ethical norm by which one could measure one's own humanity, the norm that the Compsons rejected despite the very embodiment of it (Dilsey) in their immediate presence. Mrs. Compson, Quentin, and Jason all chose to reject their humanity in favor of vanity or pride or self-pity.

When one or more of the Compsons withdrew into their narrow, separate worlds, Dilsey remained in the public world of circumstance, change, and human trial. Dilsey had no quarrel with time, with the past or with the present. By accepting whatever time brought, she was able to adjust to every new circumstance and so maintain order in the midst of the Compson disorder all around her. What's more, she realized and acted out her own humanity in a natural, graceful, and instinctive way. She had no need for a code of ethics or morality, or for any other kind of systematized philosophy or religious belief.

But the possibility does exist that she derived some substance (as well as sustenance) from attending church. If we are to judge the strength of that particular influence by her attendance at Easter service, we find that neither in her attitude nor in the service itself (according to Vickery) does she make any reference to sin and punishment. For her the service symbolizes man's efforts to survive between suffering and its surcease. She will not judge the Compsons lest she be judged herself. If they have lost the desire to attend church, so much the worse for them; Benjy, at least, is still fit to partake of the consolations of religion, even if he must receive them in a Negro church.

Emphasis on formalized religion or ritual in the novel is slight; the Easter service is the one significant ritual (although Quentin's several trips to the Branch in search of a "cleansing" for his sins is a form of baptism). As she proceeds from the Compson house to the church, she is fully conscious of her role as a Compson surrogate accepting faith for those too proud to seek it out themselves. Having been reassured by her participation in the church service, she is ready to return to the Compson household prepared to offer the occupants thereof the same old universal truths she had been offering them year after year, with the same response — total rejection.

DILSEY AND "SOUL." There is a noticeable change in language in Dilsey's section. Once again we find poetry, but of a simpler kind than that encountered in the Quentin section. It is as if we had suddenly jumped from the elegance of Edmund Spenser to the earthiness of William Wordsworth. The poetry may be found mainly in those passages which report Dilsey's reaction to the Easter service — simple but not primitive, and definitely complex and mature. The reader must determine at this point whether Dilsey's strength and virtues derive from some "mystique of race" which we now refer to as "soul." Faulkner, for his part, was not quite ready to accept that interpretation, call it what you will. He resisted the temptation to oversimplify by setting up the "good primitive black folk" against the "corrupt wicked white folk." Luster could say of the Compsons that "Dese is funny folks. Glad I ain't none of em," only to have Dilsey come back at him with "Lemme tell you somethin, nigger boy, you got jes es much Compson devilment in you es any of em" (p. 192). Of course she believes in original sin: men (white *and* black) are not "naturally" (or in the Rousseauan sense) good but need order and discipline and divine grace.

Dilsey, then, is no primitive whose goodness arises from her close contact with nature. It is not a goodness that preaches a faith in man as man. Dilsey is a complete Christian, believing in God, not in man. God's rod and His staff may comfort her; but she in turn will not hesitate to put *her* rod and staff to the task of preventing her own children from falling from grace. She is merely doing God's work. As a member of a deprived race, Dilsey may be closer to the helpful influences of religion as much through necessity as through conviction. There is a fundamentalism (non-theological, of course) in religion that keeps people (especially the deprived and the underprivileged) closer to the basic and essential values in life. Faulkner certainly believed in that since his Negro characters (see comments in next section) show "less false pride, less false idealism, and more seasoned discipline in human relationship" (Cleanth Brooks). He must have, judging by the emphasis he gave to the Easter service that Dilsey attends.

"Dilsey isn't searching for a soul. She *is* the soul," says Evelyn Scott. "She is the conscious human accepting the limitations of herself, the iron boundaries of circumstance, and still, to the best of her ability, achieving a holy compromise for aspiration." Were Evelyn Scott or anyone else writing that same statement today, the conclusion would undoubtedly be that Dilsey *had* "soul." Until a better definition of "soul" comes along, we'll accept Miss Scott's.

CADDY, BEAUTIFUL ONE, HEART'S DARLING. "I fell in love with one of my characters, Caddy," Faulkner said. "I loved her so much I couldn't decide to give her life just for the duration of the short story. She deserved more than that. So my novel was created, almost in spite of myself." What did Faulkner see in Caddy that moved him to such terms of adulation of her? For one, she was obviously the only one in a dying family who was alive. For another, she was obviously the only one who was capable and willing to give herself entirely to life and to love. To live was to love; to love was to live. All the other Compsons were self-absorbed, locked into their own private worlds. Caddy represents the life that all the other Compsons forgot to live.

CADDY: FROM LOVE TO PROMISCUITY. There is no doubt, Caddy was no paragon of virtue. More likely, she was a child of nature — honest, uninhibited, and full of the vital juices of life. In adolescence, these juices begin to flow, and Caddy *naturally* responds to love and to life. She is seventeen when Dalton Ames relieves her of "the frail physical stricture which to her was no more than a hangnail would have been." The importance she attaches to that event in her young life is not shared by the other Compsons; what may appear to be a "natural response" by more liberated members of any community is distorted into something dirty, corrupt, and a fatal reflection on the family honor. Having been made to feel the full extent of the guilt coming upon the consequence of her earlier "promiscuity" (she had let herself be kissed by a boy, an event that caused Mrs. Compson to go into a temporary state of mourning), she anticipates Dalton Ames's gesture to make her "an honest woman." But Ames refuses to marry her, and she is left pregnant and unmarried. She feels the loss of Dalton very deeply but can live with that loss except for her mother's lamentations over the family disgrace and her own sense of guilt over what she has done to Benjy and Quentin. Her love for the two boys is genuine and maternal; in the absence of a real, natural, *loving* mother, she has given them the loving care and tender attention that Mrs. Compson was unable to give them. Later on, still in love with Dalton, Caddy is ready to give herself incestuously to Quentin to help him overcome his profound anguish. "Caddy's love for her brother," Volpe believes, "is not essentially incestuous; her offer of herself is an act of abnegation, motivated by a love that is almost maternal." (An interesting observation, but valid only if one construes a sexual relationship between mother and son as non-incestuous.)

CADDY: FROM PROMISCUITY TO MARRIAGE. Caddy's experience with Dalton Ames has led her to promiscuity. She is two months pregnant by an itinerant lover when she marries Herbert Head. (Did Faulkner choose the name intentionally to underscore the contrast between Caddy as heart, passion, and Herbert Head as intellect, restraint?) Even before the fact of Caddy's pregnancy has been unalterably established, the fact of her loss of virginity is enough to impel Mrs. Compson to rush her off to French Lick, Indiana, to find her a husband. They find Herbert Head, who falls in love with Caddy (she does not return his love) and agrees to marry her (assuming she is a virgin) and to give Jason a job in a bank. The marriage takes place almost nine months after Caddy's affair with Dalton Ames, time enough for shrewd Herbert to realize that the child his wife has borne is not his (bankers usually know their arithmetic — if not their women — quite well). Caddy is forced to leave his house, but not before she has agreed to leave her baby in the care of Mrs. Compson (?) and Dilsey, with money to be sent regularly to Jason (who almost had a good job in a bank) to bank and use for the care of the child.

CADDY: "ONCE A BITCH . . ." For the rest of the Caddy story, the reader is indebted to the Appendix Faulkner provided for *The Sound and The Fury*. Caddy was divorced by Head in 1911, married to a film executive in Hollywood in 1920, divorced in Mexico in 1925. No information until 1940, when Caddy vanished in the German occupation of Paris "still beautiful and probably still wealthy too since she did not look within fifteen years of her actual forty-eight," not to be heard of again until 1943 when Melissa Meek, Jefferson librarian, came across a disturbing picture in a slick magazine. It was a picture that smacked of luxury and money — "a Cannebière backdrop of mountains and palms and cypresses and the sea, an open powerful expensive chromium-trimmed sports car, the woman's face hatless between a rich scarf and a seal coat, ageless and beautiful, cold, serene and damned; beside her a handsome lean man of middle-age in the ribbons and tabs of a German staffgeneral." Melissa, former classmate of Candace, took the picture to Jason. " 'That Candace?' " he said, " 'Don't make me laugh. This bitch ain't thirty yet. The other one's fifty now.' " *The following are worth noting:* (1) Jason refers to his sister, not as *Caddy* but as *Candace,* as if in implied respect for her unquestionable material success; (2) Caddy achieves the pinnacle of material success through her marriage to a Nazi bigwig, an implication by Faulkner (a) of the future course of the world if it should persist in its absolutely materialistic, immoral ways, and (b) the hopeless future for love in a loveless world, as exemplified by Caddy's fate. (3) Caddy was willing to give herself entirely to life and to love. (For more on Caddy, in the form of a "re-run," we shall have to wait until the section on Miss Quentin.)

CAROLINE COMPSON: SOCIAL STATUS IS EVERY-THING. Many factors contributed to the breakup of the Compson family, but the one most significant cause was the neurasthenic, self-centered mother. Caroline Compson could never forget that she was once (and would always be) a Bascomb, and everybody of course knew that the Bascombs were socially superior to the Compsons. The birth of an idiot son could not — and should not — have happened to a Bascomb; this was God's way of punishing her for having married beneath her station. To atone for this serious blunder, she abdicates her role of mother to Caddy, her role as homemaker to Dilsey, withholds any real love from her husband, Caddy, Benjy, and Quentin, and spoils (and eventually corrupts) Jason, who is more of a Bascomb than a Compson (she thinks).

Mrs. Compson is not really wicked or evil; she is merely negative, and it is her negativity which insidiously corrupts the normal family relationships. She is very likely the cause of her husband's retreat into alcohol and cynicism, the unwilling but nonetheless effective "castrator" of Quentin, and is also very probably at the root of Caddy's promiscuity.

Mrs. Compson's major preoccupation in life was to convince everybody around her that she was in every respect a Southern lady; as such, she was to be considered a *non-participating* member of the Compson family.

MRS. COMPSON AND QUENTIN. Mrs. Compson is a hypochondriac forever retreating into her bedroom enclave with psychosomatic headaches probably caused by her own rejection of motherhood, sex, and her regressive longing for the ideal of virginity. She is always calling upon Dilsey to support her self-indulgence and self-pity. Her effect on Quentin as he was growing up is documented in great detail in his recollections of the past. "If I only had a mother," he says several times during that fatal last day. He recalls associating his mother with a picture in one of his books: "a dark place into which a single weak ray of light came slanting upon two faces lifted out of the shadow" (p. 191). Quentin immediately substitutes the faces of his father and mother for those in the picture. From time to time he would be drawn back to the picture until "the dungeon was Mother herself she and Father upward into weak light holding hands and us lost somewhere below even then without a ray of light." He remembers his mother in these more significant words: "Done in Mother's mind though. Finished. Finished. Then we were all poisoned" (p. 121).

MRS. COMPSON AND BENJAMIN. (She never called him Benjy.) Mrs. Compson in her own way is as religious as Dilsey. But, whereas Dilsey expects to be punished by God for sins committed wittingly *and* unwittingly, Mrs. Compson fancies herself, like Job, the innocent victim of an undiscriminating, power-hungry God. Following her own narrow interpretation of Puritan theology, she renames her youngest son Benjamin (the name in Hebrew literally means "youngest son") in order to dramatize what she considers a curse on the Compsons and, more particularly, on herself for her "sin," marrying a Compson. The idiot son is God's "judgment" visited on her; how much more proper then, to take the Bascomb name of Maury from the idiot boy and replace it with the name of Benjamin.

MRS. COMPSON AND JASON. For some time Mrs. Compson felt sure that she had not produced an idiot child (God was responsible for the child; in His inscrutable way, that was the form that His judgment would take). Since there was no evading the fact of the child, she then decided (against her husband's wishes) to change the child's name from Maury to Benjamin, thereby freeing herself of the responsibility, but more important than that, separating Benjy from the Bascombs. She then alienates herself from Caddy — easily done, since Caddy's "promiscuous" tendencies as a girl and her eventual "fall from grace" provide Mrs. Compson with a "legitimate," moral excuse — and from Quentin, who is too much of a romantic Compson after all. In this way she successfully divides the family into Bascombs and Compsons, with herself, her brother Maury (why did she name her youngest child "Maury" in the first place?), and her son Jason in opposition to Mr. Compson and the other children. With Jason, she shares those values that are in sharp contradistinction to traditional and social values that Mr. Compson and his son Quentin represent. She and Jason place greater value on appearances than on moral integrity. Throughout her long, whining existence, Mrs. Compson finds reassurance and comfort in Jason; and when he is the only child who turns out as she wanted, he is a most accurate male counterpart of the kind of woman Mrs. Compson is.

MRS. COMPSON AND "LITTLE MOTHER CADDY." So far as motherly love is concerned, Quentin, Caddy, and Benjy all suffer from emotional deprivation. Caddy tries to meet the deficiency in Quentin by offering him a kind of love that lies somewhere between motherly and sisterly love. The effort fails; moreover, it is safe to assume that much of Quentin's disgust with his own emerging sexuality is related to the selfsame emotional deprivation he experienced as a child.

Caddy seeks the remedy for her emotional deprivation in a precocious sexuality, then in a promiscuous sexuality, and finally in a serial monogamy (marriage-divorce-marriage, etc.). Benjy has no way of knowing he is suffering from emotional deprivation; for him there was always Caddy (until she married and left), or one of Caddy's old slippers, or the smell of trees. Mrs. Compson meant nothing to Benjy; if he could identify his mother, he would probably name Caddy. Caddy supplies the love that Mrs. Compson actively denies Quentin and Benjy. Jason needs no love, not even that of Mrs. Compson.

**MR. JASON COMPSON III: UNCOMFORTABLE CYNIC.** By 1910, two years before his death, Mr. Compson was a defeated man. To most people he had always seemed a weak man, overintellectual, lacking guts to fight the many forces threatening his possessions and his family. He sold off part of the Compson land too soon (he needed the money to pay for Quentin at Harvard and for Caddy's wedding), not because it was an easy decision to make but because he felt for both Quentin and Caddy.

Despite the facile, cynical way in which he dismissed Caddy's seduction by Dalton Ames, he was a man of love and compassion, and strongly felt the impact of Caddy's wantonness. When Quentin recalls his father's remarks about women and virginity, he probably does not realize it was Mr. Compson's only way of softening the blow for Quentin and for himself.

**MR. COMPSON AND QUENTIN.** In one or two instances Benjy says that both Quentin and his father "smelled of rain." The observation is important in that it shows how Benjy instinctively recognized what so many others in the family consciously perceived: Quentin was very close to his father, and so much like him that the influence of his father on him was apparently very powerful. One should note how thoroughly saturated Quentin's section is with references and observations that Father used and made. The phrase "Father said" almost becomes a *leitmotif* for the section, as Quentin recalls illustration after illustration of his father's wisdom.

MR. COMPSON AND ILLUSION OF VICTORY. Among several causes of Mr. Compson's ineffectiveness as a father, husband, and man may be included the effect on his self-confidence (his *machismo*, if you will) of his knowledge he had fathered an idiot son. The Caddy-Dalton Ames affair did not help either; did Caddy stray because of the inadequate male image he had afforded her in her formative years? Since he was a thinking man, none of these conjectures (and others) could be overlooked by him.

Mr. Compson's cynicism, then, was more of a "protective" philosophy than a retreat from reality or responsibility. He tells Quentin (after the Ames affair: ". . . every man is the arbiter of his own virtues but let no man prescribe for another man's wellbeing . . ." (p. 221). Don't try to impose moral convictions upon life . . . reality cannot measure up to such values . . . values themselves are meaningless. Yes, even virginity is useless, a very temporary (and probably unnecessary) condition, as valueless as all human conditions set down by man to meet societal needs. Man-made values are not absolutes, nothing in life is so stable as to resist forever the destructive force of time. Time is the tyrant; and this Quentin readily accepts. One need only note Quentin's obsessive preoccupation with time throughout the second section of the novel. Mr. Compson tells Quentin to stop resisting time because "no battle is ever won. . . . They are not even fought. The field only reveals to man his own folly and despair, and victory is an illusion of philosophers and fools" (p. 95).

MR. COMPSON AND THE HEART OF DARKNESS. Quentin would still like to fight the useless battles, despite his father's cautions. He thinks he can overcome the shame

of Caddy, of himself, of the whole family, by pretending
that it was he, not Dalton Ames, who had had sexual relations with Caddy. But his father won't accept the feeble lie.
". . . you wanted to sublimate a piece of natural human folly
into a horror and then exorcise it with truth," the father
tells him (p. 220). Quentin next suggests that suicide would
be the best way out of the enormous moral dilemma in which
he finds himself. That won't work either, his father tells
him: ". . . you are not thinking of finitude you are contemplating an apotheosis in which a temporary state of mind
will become symmetrical above the flesh it will not quite
discard you will not even be dead . . ." (p. 220). Through Mr.
Compson, Faulkner leads us (says Frederick Hoffman)
"beyond the familiar levels of experience and forces us to
look unflinchingly into the darkness." This is in strong contradistinction to the Faulkner who once said it was better to
live a full life than to write. But if one must write at the
expense of leading the more desirable full life, then one
must feel obligated to take the lead, at every opportunity,
in the struggle, in the "impossible" battles, even fighting
alone, if necessary, in the effort to transcend the boundaries
of life, the man-made ones and the natural ones. In Mr.
Compson, however, Faulkner found an intellectual position
that was too articulate and attractive to resist.

NOBODY LOVED MISS QUENTIN. Except for Dilsey,
who naturally felt for the deprived and the underprivileged,
nobody really loved Miss Quentin. True, Caddy sent money
regularly for the support of her child, and once even paid
Jason an exorbitant sum just to catch a fleeting glance of
the girl, but she managed quite well miles away from her
daughter.

One might have expected the author himself to show some
compassion and understanding of the wayward child of
wayward parents. Instead, he describes Miss Quentin's room
after she has left with Jason's money as follows (note the

loaded words, herein underlined by us, that he uses) : "It was *not* a girl's room. It was not anybody's room, and the faint scent of *cheap* cosmetics and the few feminine objects and the other evidences of *crude* and *hopeless* efforts to feminize it but added to its *anonymity,* giving it that *dead* and *stereotyped* transcience of rooms in *assignation houses.* The bed had not been disturbed. On the floor lay a *soiled* undergarment of *cheap silk a little too pink;* from a half open bureau dangled a single stocking . . ." (p. 352).

Nor did Grandmother Compson show much more sympathy for the child who had run away from a home in which she had never been shown any real affection. "It's in the blood. Like uncle, like niece," she said, meaning not Uncle Jason but Uncle Quentin. Quentin had also affronted her by taking his own life just because he didn't have the guts to face reality as Jason did. "Or mother," Mrs. Compson added. "I don't know which would be worse. I don't seem to care," and asked Dilsey for her Bible (p. 374). First Benjy, then Caddy, then Quentin, and now Miss Quentin; would the Lord ever stop visiting the afflictions of Job upon her?

But Jason had the least reason of all for loving Miss Quentin. "The bitch that cost me a job, the one chance I ever had to get ahead," he lamented, recalling how Head had changed his mind about giving Jason the job in the bank once he found out that Caddy was to give birth to a bastard child. ". . . that killed my father and is shortening my mother's life every day and made my name a laughing stock in the town . . ." (p. 379). The filial concern is questionable; the actual loss of real money is not. Not only had Miss Quentin absconded with a considerable sum of money (much of which Jason could not legally claim), but her departure had abruptly cut off a regular source of revenue for Jason, namely, the money Caddy remitted with admirable regularity for Miss Quentin's support.

LIKE MOTHER, LIKE DAUGHTER — NOT QUITE. The loss of money bothered Jason considerably, but not as much as the fact that he had been outwitted by a woman, a girl, "a bitch." It would have been so much easier to sustain the loss if he could believe that it was Miss Quentin's companion, the carnival man, who had robbed him. He must track the two scoundrels down, see them first, get the money back, then let them go. He must do nothing to let the whole world (Jefferson and Mottson, at least) know that he, Jason Compson, "had been robbed by Quentin, his niece, a bitch." Jason was certain Caddy would never come to any good, nor would her daughter. Nor did the daughter have the same talents as her mother; the pattern would never be completely repeated. As Faulkner put it in the Appendix, "And so vanished; whatever occupation overtook her would have arrived in no chromium Mercedes; whatever snapshot would have contained no general of staff" (p. 426). For Faulkner, at least, Caddy was a *nonpareil.*

# FAULKNER AND THE CRITICS

It was Malcolm Cowley who virtually "resurrected" William Faulkner as a major American writer in 1946 with his editorship of *The Portable Faulkner*. Faulkner was "unknown" before that date except as the author of the sensational novel, *Sanctuary*, despite the fact that he had already written twelve novels, two collections of short stories (*These 13*, 1931; *Doctor Martino and Other Stories*, 1934), and two collections of poems (*The Marble Faun*, 1924; *A Green Bough*, 1933) — all published! How "unknown" can a writer get? Cowley led the way; awarding of the Nobel Prize for Literature to Faulkner in 1950 increased the critical momentum; and today there is a considerable body of Faulkner criticism available for those who would learn more about one of America's very bad-very good writers.

## *General Criticism*

PRICE AND THE QUOTABLE FAULKNER. Writing in 1972, Reynolds Price observed that "Faulkner, after decades of neglect, has swollen and will probably assuage until we see him again as a very deep but narrow trench, not the Great Meteor Crater he now seems to many." On the other hand, Price, in comparing Faulkner with Hemingway ("For Ernest Hemingway," *New American Review* 14), found Faulkner eminently more quotable. "Hemingway, unlike Faulkner," he wrote, "is always badly served by spot-quotations, as anyone will know who turns from critical discussions of him (with their repertoire of a dozen Great Paragraphs) back to the works themselves. Faulkner, so often shortwinded, can be flattered by brief citation, shown at the stunning moment of triumph." It is rather strange to see Faulkner referred to as a "sprinter," rather than the lonely "long-distance runner" described by Clifton Fadiman and others. What Price is probably suggesting is that Faulkner is incapable of *sustained* brilliance, that he can be extremely flashy between sieges of sesquipedalian prose.

**HEMINGWAY ON FAULKNER.** In 1932, Paul Romaine was preparing a small anthology of some of Faulkner's early works, mainly those which had first appeared in the New Orleans *Double Dealer*. In order to make the collection salesworthy, Romaine wanted to include Hemingway's little poem, "Ultimately" (it had appeared in the June, 1922, number of the *Double Dealer* alongside a piece of prose by "an obscure young Mississippian named William Faulkner") on the back cover. Hemingway agreed, although he told his bibliographer, Captain Cohn, in strictest confidence, that "the poem was bad enough to fit perfectly into a collection of Faulkner's 'early shit' " (quoted by Carlos Baker, *Ernest Hemingway: A Life Story*). Hemingway also remarked to Owen Wister that although he liked *As I Lay Dying*, he thought that *Sanctuary* was "pretty phoney."

Hemingway's relationship with Faulkner was a hate-love one. To James Farrell, then a promising young writer, Hemingway remarked that "Faulkner was a far better writer than either himself or Farrell." That was in 1936, after a considerable amount of wine had been consumed. In 1944, Hemingway magnanimously admitted to Jean-Paul Sartre that Faulkner was a better writer than he.

But Hemingway's magnanimity apparently ran out in 1951, when (Carlos Baker reports) "his first ungrudging reaction to Faulkner's Nobel Prize was spoiled by his assertion that he was proud of not writing like the author of the latest installment of the 'Octonawhoopoo' story in the *Partisan Review*." The publication of *A Fable* in 1954 confirmed still another of Hemingway's peculiar theories about writers. Hemingway believed that "no son of a bitch that ever won the Nobel Prize ever wrote anything worth reading afterwards," and maintained that the false and con-

trived nature of *A Fable* confirmed his theory. Faulkner's
latest book showed, said Hemingway, that "all a man needed,
in order to do 5,000 words a day of that kind of stuff, was
a quart of whiskey, the loft of a barn, and a total disregard
of syntax" (Baker's version).

When "Old Corndrinking Mellifluous'" (Hemingway's
playful epithet for Faulkner) short-story collection, *Big
Woods,* came out in 1955, Hemingway is reported to have
told Faulkner that the stories were expertly written (Hemingway, who was basically a magnificent short-story writer,
could recognize a similar excellence in Faulkner), carefully
perceived, but that he (Hemingway) "would have been more
moved if Mr. Faulkner had ever hunted animals that ran
both ways" (Baker's version). Hemingway's definitive critique on Faulkner went something like this: *Sanctuary* and
*Pylon,* very readable; *The Bear* commands attention; some
of the Negro "stuff," very good; *A Fable,* not even worthy
of a place at Ichang, where they shipped the night soil from
Chungking.

ALLEN TATE RATES FAULKNER. "Leaving aside the
two books that I have not read [one is *The Reivers*], I should
say that he wrote at least five masterpieces (What other
American novelist wrote so many, except James?) : they
are *The Sound and The Fury, As I Lay Dying, Sanctuary,
Light in August, and The Hamlet*" (as quoted in Robert
Penn Warren's *Faulkner, A Collection of Critical Essays*).
Tate was almost inclined to add to the list *The Wild Palms*
and *Absalom, Absalom!,* but in the end concluded that despite some very great writing in them, they still did not
add up to being novels (a running argument, joined in by
Cowley and others, on whether Faulkner wrote *real* novels
or clusters of related short stories). Tate further emphasized that all of Faulkner's seven great books, plus *The Bear,*
were written within a span of eleven or twelve years. He
also agreed with Hemingway (and others) that Faulkner

wrote "only one bad novel, *A Fable,* his version of the Grand Inquisitor, conceived in theological ignorance and placed in a setting he had not observed. . . ."

One other characteristic about Faulkner bothered Tate, who, on the whole, must be considered among Faulkner's "friendly" critics. That was Faulkner's snobbishness, or an irrational dedication to a gentility that the English long since had abandoned, and that the Old South may never have actually possessed. "Years ago," Tate reports, "when I was editing *The Sewanee Review,* I had some correspondence with him; his letters were signed 'Faulkner.' I wrote him that English nobility followed this practice and I never heard from him again" (reported in Warren). Tate's observation of Faulkner's affection (and affectation) for the English is substantially corroborated in the several instances of Quentin's fawning admiration of the Blands (in the second section of *The Sound and The Fury*), and in John Faulkner's comments on his brother Bill's unending love for clothes and customs English (*My Brother Bill,* pp. 116-118, 123-124, 125).

HOWE ON FAULKNER AS MALE CHAUVINIST. There is a considerable amount of evidence in Faulkner's writing to indicate that he was either downright misogynistic or very uncomfortable in his treatment of female characters. Warren quotes Howe as saying that "Faulkner's inability to achieve moral depth in his portraiture of young women clearly indicates a major failing as a novelist. It is an instance where his reliance on the folk imagination, fruitful though it usually is, plays him false. . . ."

FIEDLER ON FAULKNER AS MALE CHAUVINIST. Fiedler goes far beyond Howe in making the same allegation. He observes (in "William Faulkner: Highbrow's Lowbrow," *No, in Thunder!*) that "In the work of William Faulkner, the fear of the castrating woman and the dis-ease with sexuality present in the novels of his contempories, Fitzgerald and Hemingway, attain their fullest and shrillest expressions. . . . In no other writer in the world do pejorative stereotypes of women appear with greater frequency and on more levels, from the most trivial to the most profound. . . ."

COUGHLAN ON FAULKNER'S "THEATER OF CRUELTY." It is possible, according to Robert Coughlan (*The Private World of William Faulkner*), that Faulkner's "disease" with sexuality and women is a manifestation of a deeply imbedded streak of sadism. "In Faulkner's writing," Coughlan observes, "life has no meaning except to the individual. There is no moral law beyond what in an older day might have been called 'the code of the gentleman' — 'courage and honor and pride, and pity and love of justice and of liberty'; but to keep this code brings no rewards beyond self-respect — it brings no salvation, no protection, for the 'good' and 'bad' characters are damned impartially to futility, and often to physical and mental tortures so macabre and so vividly conveyed that they seem to reflect sadism in the writer." The analogy with Artaud's "theater of cruelty" is most vividly displayed in the rare exceptions that Faulkner makes, usually for villains like Jason Compson in *The Sourd and The Fury* and Flem Snopes in *The Hamlet*. These are "bad" men, cruel and avaricious, who are permitted to triumph over what has been called (old-fashioned though it may be) virtue.

HAMILTON ON FAULKNER'S IDEA OF EXPIATION. In reviewing Faulkner's *Requiem for a Nun* (*The Saturday Review*, July 12, 1952), Edith Hamilton accuses Faulkner both of having contradicted the noblest of sentiments expressed in his Nobel Prize speech a year earlier and of having endorsed in his latest book the thesis that the end justifies the means, "that ancient falsehood which has been the cause of the most hateful deeds men have done to each other." In this book, as in so many of his other books, Faulkner, she maintains, preaches that men of themselves "can wipe out evil and achieve goodness if they are willing to torture themselves. They do not need forgiveness." If the sinner suffers enough, then the sin can be expiated, the debt thereby incurred to God can be wiped out. Faulkner, moreover, is preaching (Miss Hamilton continues) "not that a crime is pardonable, but that it is admirable, if it is seen by the criminal as the only way to stop another crime conceived of as greater." Thus, when Nancy, the Negro, strangles Temple's baby because she can conceive of no other more effective way of stopping Temple from eloping with a blackmailer and a thief, Nancy is exalted by her deed to a level higher than that occupied by the others — she becomes the Nun of the story. And that way, Miss Hamilton concludes, lies a rejection of God, an endorsement of sadism and of a morality worthy of what Maxwell Geismar insists upon calling Fascism.

GEISMAR ON FAULKNER'S REJECTION OF THE DEMOCRATIC CREDO. To Maxwell Geismar, Faulkner's writing, in large part, must be considered in the larger tradition of "reversionary, neopagan, and neurotic discontent" from which Fascism arises. Faulkner's novels seem to him to be part of the "anti-civilized revolt arising out of modern social evils, nourished by ignorance of their true nature, and which succumbs to malice as their solution" (quoted by Coughlan, *op. cit.*). Faulkner is at his best, says Geismar, when he is exploring and illustrating "the typical phobias and deep, haunting fears and obsessions of the cultural background whose supreme literary voice he really is." Faulkner is the literary historian of the negative — of decaying, incestuous aristocrats in *The Sound and The Fury*, and the tortured mulatto hero, Joe Christmas, who embodies the buried fears and terrors in the Southern psyche even as he struggles to determine his own identity, only to become the lover and then the murderer of the white woman who has led him on to rape her in her sexual fantasies (*Light in August*). "These are Faulkner's great and permanent achievements," says Geismar (*The Saturday Review*, July 12, 1952) — "these shadows, swamps, morasses, and psychic quicksands of the still-haunted mind of the South which he knows so surely and so intuitively. . . ."

FAULKNER, HAWTHORNE OF THE SOUTH. Thus far, we have presented a most powerful indictment of Faulkner, not so much as a novelist, but as a moralist. According to Cleanth Brooks (*William Faulkner: The Yoknapatawpha Country*), we may have joined Tate, Howe, Fiedler, Coughlan, Hamilton, and Geismar in making the mistake of taking Faulkner's fiction to be sociology — "an amateur and nonacademic sociology characterized by powerful moral overtones. There is in such criticism," Brooks points out, "a surreptitious commerce between sociological-historical fact and fictional meaning. Particular insights and moral judgments . . . are smuggled across the frontier into the realm of historical fact and become generalizations about Southern culture." For the moment, let us examine the kind of critical approach to Faulkner that Brooks would endorse — Cowley's comparison of Faulkner with Nathaniel Hawthorne (Introduction, *The Portable Faulkner*):

> . . . *Hawthorne had much the same attitude toward New England that Faulkner has to the South, together with a strong sense of regional particularity. The Civil War made Hawthorne feel that "the North and the South were two distinct nations in opinions and habits, and had better not try to live under the same institutions"* . . . *Like Faulkner in the South, he applied himself to creating its moral fables and elaborating its legends, which existed, as it were, in his solitary heart.* . . .
> *Faulkner is another author who has to wait for the spirit and the voice. He is not so much a novelist, in the usual sense of being a writer who set out to observe actions and characters, then fits them into the frame-*

*work of a story, as he is an epic or bardic poet in prose,*
*a creator of myths that he weaves together into a legend*
*of the South.*

BROOKS' STRICTURES. Faulkner is "a creator of myths
that he weaves together into a legend of the South," not a
recorder of "particular insights and moral judgments" for
amateur and nonacademic sociologists to convert into historical "facts" to prove (says Brooks) "the accuracy of the
sweeping judgments of the Southern scene that are attrib-
uted to Faulkner. . . . Most authors of Faulkner criticism
are serious moralists, and they recognize that Faulkner is,
in his own way, a moralist too. They want to take him seriously and this means that they are very much concerned
with the factual substratum of Faulkner's mythical country." Be that as it may, Brooks's strictures will not deter
the critics from digging into the factual substratum of
Faulkner's mythical country or from digging into the factual substratum of Faulkner's esthetic morality. "What is
of basic concern here," Brooks insists, "is what is always
of concern in literature: the relation of truth of fact to
aesthetic value — of 'truth of reference' to 'truth of co-
herence'." The mistake many of Faulkner's critics make is
to confuse the validity of a piece of fiction with the validity
of a fact. If the fiction is creditable (*not* necessarily credible), they say, then the "facts" must be correct; conversely,
if the facts are incorrect, then the fiction must be poor. But
Faulkner is primarily an artist, and as such he is interested
in creating the best novels and stories of which he is capable; if, incidentally, these same pieces of fiction tell something about the South, then that is an added increment,
earned by the reader only if he is prepared to read these
novels and stories with the kind of discrimination that will
help him see what Faulkner is doing with *his* "facts." In
short, no one (save an Oscar Wilde, perhaps) should expect
an artist to be absolutely amoral; by the same token, no
one should expect a great artist to be an *explicit* moralist.

## Criticism of Style

*"Agonizing prose which appears to be chewed like tobacco and occasionally squirted out, instead of being written" (V. S. Pritchett).*

*"Perhaps the most elaborate, intermittently incoherent and ungrammatical, thunderous, polyphonic rhetoric in all American writing (Alfred Kazin).*

*"[Faulkner's method is] Anti-Narrative, a set of complex devices used to keep the story from being told . . . as if a child were to go to work on it with a pair of shears" (Clifton Fadiman).*

RANSOM ON FAULKNER AS JOHN WEBSTER. "The books of this writer are unequal, and the style is less than consistently sustained," observes John Crowe Ransom, who sees in Faulkner, not Ben Jonson, not Shakespeare, but the John Webster of *The Duchess of Malfi, The White Devil,* and other Elizabethan horror plays. Ransom makes the comparison on the basis of "the face of his [Faulkner's] horror, as in the rightness of his sense of human goodness, as in the gift of a language which is generally adequate to the effects intended" (as quoted by Warren). Ransom's criticism of Faulkner's style is not quite as destructive as the first three quoted, but it is still less than unqualified, more of a polite, Southern "soft impeachment." However, it will do until we find a more favorable one. Before that, let us file a few more minority reports.

WILSON ON HYPER-PARENTHETICAL FAULKNER. "It would require a good deal of very diligent work . . . always to turn out the combinations of words that would do what Faulkner wants them to do. His energy, his image-making genius get him where he wants to go about seventy per cent of the time, but when he misses it, he lands in a mess." So far, so good; seventy per cent represents a more than favorable evaluation of Faulkner's achievement. But what really "bugs" Wilson most — aside from Faulkner's shifting of the syntax in the middle of a sentence and to his concatenating of long sequences of clauses with hardly any syntax at all — is "his inserting in parenthesis in the middle of a scene (in one case, in the middle of a sentence) a long episode that took place at some other time, to his invention of the punctuation (( )) to indicate a parenthesis within a parenthesis or to his creation of non-dictionary words" (*Classics and Commercials*).

Wilson's appreciation of Faulkner's "image-making genius" is understandable, since Wilson was one of the first of the strong supporters of the French Symbolists (Faulkner's favorites, too). His impatience with some of Faulkner's unsyntactical prose is equally understandable in a writer himself of such pellucid prose. The exception he takes to the "non-dictionary words" does not hold up under a close examination of a good unabridged dictionary. Finally, the disapproval of Faulkner's constant "scene-shifting" (was he referring particularly to *The Sound and The Fury*, perhaps?) shows an insensitivity to what Conrad Aiken has called "the novel as form" (which we shall examine a little later). Having dealt with so many other literary innovators in his long, distinguished career as a critic, Wilson should have known that the form follows the content.

DE VOTO VOTES "NO." "When a narrative sentence has to have as many as three parentheses identifying the reference of pronouns," De Voto says, referring of course to a different use of the parenthesis from that criticized by Wilson, "it signifies mere bad writing and can be justified by no psychological or esthetic principle whatever." (Quotation from Coughlan, *op. cit.*) Clear and blunt.

HOWE AND THE ROAD TO OBSCURITY. ". . . he sometimes drove too hard, sometimes fell into obscurity." Faulkner did, of course, and no honest critic or reader can deny that there are patches or prose of such a deep purple at times to suggest that Faulkner was probably "driving by night." But Howe generally gives Faulkner good marks (almost equal to Wilson's seventy per cent), and suggests that when he succeeds — and that is more often than not — "the result is marvelously rich, a full expression of the way an experience feels, the way a relationship moves, the way a human being responds at one and the same time to the pressures of his outer life and the needs of his inner life" (*Major Writers of America*).

BECK ON FAULKNER'S USE OF THE COLLOQUIAL. To Beck, Faulkner is not all rich, metaphorical, symbolic language. At times, says Beck, "there exists in almost all of Faulkner's work a realistic colloquialism, expressing lively dialogue that any playwright might envy" — say, for example, a John Webster? — "and even carrying over into sustained first-person narrative the flavor of regionalism and the idiosyncracies of character" — say, for example, Jason Compson, in the third section of *The Sound and The Fury*? "In the colloquial vein," Beck concludes, "Faulkner's brilliance is unsurpassed in contemporary American fiction" (*William Faulkner's Style*).

WILSON ON FAULKNER'S PROVINCIALITY. Wilson, as indicated earlier, is on the whole a friendly critic. As such, he offers a rather interesting (not necessarily new, since Cowley had already remarked on Faulkner's resemblance to Hawthorne; and, as we shall learn from Faulkner himself, he was very much aware of the influence Wilson speaks of) explanation for Faulkner's uniquely difficult style. He says:

> But the weaknesses of Faulkner . . . have their origin in the antiquated community he inhabits, for they result from his not having mastered — I speak of the design of his books as wholes as well as of that of his sentences and paragraphs — the discipline of the Joyces, Prousts and Conrads. . . . If you are going to do embroidery, you have to watch every stitch; . . . The technique of

*the modern novel, with its ideal of technical efficiency, its specialization of means for ends, has grown up in the industrial age, and it has . . . a good deal in common with . . . other manifestations of that age. In practicing it so far from such cities as produced the Flauberts, Joyces and Jameses, Faulkner's provinciality, stubbornly cherished and turned into an asset, inevitably tempts him to be slipshod and has apparently made it impossible for him to acquire complete expertness in an art that demands . . . closest attention and care* (Classics and Commercials).

FAULKNER AGREES WITH WILSON. Before quoting Faulkner, the reader should be reminded that Wilson wrote the above criticism of Faulkner in October of 1948. Faulkner's "reply" is taken from a letter by him to Malcolm Cowley written in January of 1946. (Time, as you can see, shifts for others besides Faulkner.) Faulkner wrote: "The style, as you divine, is a result of the solitude, and granted a bad one. It was further complicated by an inherited regional or geographical (Hawthorne would say, racial) curse. You might say, studbook style: by Southern Rhetoric out of Solitude or Oratory out of Solitude."

AIKEN: ONE POET TO ANOTHER. Aiken is able to see in Faulkner certain mannerisms of the poet not too successfully suppressed by Faulkner in his prose. He says of Faulkner's quasi-poetic prose that it is "like a jungle of rank creepers and ferocious blooms taking shape before one's eyes — magnificently and endlessly intervolved, glistening and ophidianly in motion, coil sliding over coil, and leaf and flower forever magically interchanging" (*The Novel As Form*). A passage worthy of Faulkner himself! Aiken also perceives in Faulkner's style "the whole elaborate method of *deliberately withheld* meaning, of progressive and partial and delayed disclosure." Or what Faulkner himself called "writing on the oblique, seein' the thing through reflections." Again, for better or worse, another mannerism or characteristic of the poetic style as applied to narrative prose. The result is often the obscurity, the involved, formless style, the endless sentences. . . . "I'm trying to say it all in one sentence," Faulkner explained (letter to Malcolm Cowley, November 1944), "between one Cap and one period. I'm still trying to put it all, if possible, on one pinhead. I don't know how to do it. All I know to do is to keep on trying in a new way. . . ." In yet another part of the same letter, Faulkner said, "I am telling the same story over and over, which is myself and the world."

AIKEN: MORE ON THE NOVEL AS FORM. ". . . Mr. Faulkner could say with Henry James that it is practically impossible to make any real distinction between theme and form." The reference to Henry James as a possible key to the "mystery" of Faulkner's style is probably more valuable than the earlier reference to Hawthorne. Aiken speaks of the pleasure that Faulkner derives from "his continuous preoccupation with the novel *as form,* his passionate concern with it, and a degree of success with it which would clearly have commanded the interest and respect of Henry James himself. The novel as revelation, the novel as slice-of-life, the novel as mere story, do not interest him: these he would say, like James again, 'are the circumstances of the interest,' but not the interest itself. The interest itself will be the use to which these circumstances are put, the degree to which they can be organized" (*The Novel As Form.*)

## Criticism of *The Sound and The Fury*

FADIMAN ON FAULKNER'S NON-STOP SENTENCE. "The first two and a half pages . . . consist of seven sentences, composed of 123, 155, 9 (something went wrong here), 146, 66, 93, and 135 words respectively. Average: 104." The book being criticized was *Absalom, Absalom!* Equally long sentences may be found in *The Sound and The Fury.* "To penetrate Mr. Faulkner's sentences is like hacking your way through a jungle," Fadiman continued. "The path closes up at once behind you, and in no time at all you find yourself entangled in a luxurious mass of modifiers, qualifications, relative clauses, parenthetical phrases, interjected matter, recapitulations, and other indications of a Great Style. All of Mr. Faulkner's shuddery inventions pale in horrendousness before the mere notion of parsing him." And this was said by a man who had edited Henry James, no more of a *parsed master* than Faulkner himself! "One day Bill said," John Faulkner writes in his gentle memoir, *My Brother Bill*, "that the next book he published was going to have a full page of periods inserted in the back with a note that if any one felt Bill had used too few periods they were free to take as many as they wished from the extra page and put in their own." We do not know whether Fadiman was eager to accept such an offer. "Seriously," he said, "I do not know what to say of this book [*Absalom, Absalom!*] except that it seems to point to the final blowup of what was once a remarkable, if minor, talent." This, in 1936!

*THE SOUND AND THE FURY* BEFORE 1946. Faulkner's fourth novel (the second in the Yoknapatawpha series) was published in 1,789 copies on October 7, 1929, a mere two weeks before the historic Wall Street Crash. The book enjoyed two smaller printings in 1931, mainly on the notoriety of Faulkner's next novel, *Sanctuary*. For more than ten years, the publishers were satisfied with an offer of less than 3,300 copies to the American public. By the time *The Sound and The Fury* was to be republished in 1946, it had been out of print for several years. Even Faulkner himself did not have a copy around, and had to write the Appendix to the novel from memory.

Aside from the fact that American readers are generally unfavorably disposed toward innovative or experimental writing, it is also very likely that the book's initially poor reception was partly due to the era of crisis and doubt during which it appeared. Faulkner's tale of a small-town South-

ern family with delusions of aristocratic glory was hardly
an uplifting piece of fiction, certainly not for a country still
reeling from unprecedented economic and social disasters.
In such an atmosphere, few readers had the patience to
plow through "jumbled time sequences, involuted narrative
structures, mangled syntax, and tortuous diction" (Irving
Howe). What they needed (they thought) was an inspira-
tional, "muscular gospel of political action and reform," not
what Lionel Trilling called in 1931 an "essentially parochial"
psychological analysis of a family in decay.

COMPSONS — "NIGHTMARE GROUP." Some early re-
viewers went beyond Trilling and accused Faulkner of having created a "nightmare group" of characters — an alcoholic, cynical father; a demanding, hypochondriac mother; a
daughter disowned for having given birth to a bastard;
and three awfully peculiar sons: a helpless idiot, an obses-
sion-driven suicide, a vicious two-bit materialist; and a
black "Mammy" running the whole gang. There was no
doubt in the minds of these critics that the young novelist
was a decadent Southerner who reveled in the manipulation
of such pathological material. They seemed even more secure in their evaluation of Faulkner when he added Temple
Drake and Popeye (*Sanctuary*) to his "nightmare group"
in 1931. Henry Seidel Canby, for one, was now convinced
that *Sanctuary* was *the* center of "the cult of cruelty."
(Strangely enough, few of the early critics recognized *As I
Lay Dying* as a logical bridge between *The Sound and The
Fury* and *Sanctuary*.)

PROPHET WITHOUT HONOR. If there were few friendly
critics among the Americans, *The Sound and The Fury*
found several friends among the more "sophisticated" Euro-
peans. The English critic, L. A. G. Strong, said that "in
conception and execution this novel has that kind of new-
ness, and gives that shock to the imagination, which puts
its author in the running for the highest stakes." Strong

was soon joined by such major French critics as André Malraux, Maurice le Breton, Maurice Coindreau, and Jean-Paul Sartre. The latter set the favorable tone with his highly impressive essay on the theme of time in *The Sound and The Fury*, and Coindreau translated the novel into French. By 1946, a new post-Depression, post-war generation was available to receive the Modern Library edition and to analyze and appreciate it within the proper social and esthetic context. Falkner's *The Sound and The Fury* had a second birth, one not to be denied.

"Did I tell you what Jean-Paul Sartre said about your work?," Malcolm Cowley asked Faulkner, in a letter dated August 9, 1945. ". . . he says that his work is based on qualities he learned from American literature. What he said about you was 'Pour les jeunes en France, Faulkner c'est un dieu.' " (Translation: "For French youth, Faulkner is a god.")

*THE SOUND AND THE FURY*: MAN AGAINST THE WALL. Another early critic, Abbott Martin, said that *The Sound and The Fury* was as "full of terror as a Greek tragedy." Other critics have likewise been inclined to see the disintegration and fall of the House of Compson as analogous to the tragedies of important families in the Old Testament, Greek and Elizabethan drama, and 19th-century novels, especially *The Brothers Karamazov*. *The Sound and The Fury* is, however, neither purely "modern" nor purely "traditional": if it reverberates with echoes of the ancient Greek and Shakespeare, it also suggests, in such figures like Maury Bascomb and names like Herbert Head and Gerald Bland (characteronymics?), characters right out of novels by Dickens and Balzac. But it is in the impact of tragedy on real people that *The Sound and The Fury* qualifies to take its place among the three or four American novels written since the late 1890's that are memorable for their analysis of the American mind and soul. *The Sound and The Fury*, observes

Irving Howe (*Faulkner: A Critical Study*), "is the one novel in which his [Faulkner's] vision and techniques are almost in complete harmony, and the vision itself whole and major. . . . In *The Sound and The Fury* Faulkner persuades us, as never before, to accept Yoknapatawpha as an emblem of a larger world beyond. . . . This book is a lament for the passing of a world. . . . Whether taken as a study of the potential for human self-destruction, or as a rendering of the social disorder particular to our time, the novel projects a radical image of man against the wall."

## Faulkner and the Blacks

In *The Sound and The Fury,* Dilsey is the last of Faulkner's Blacks who can still believe that the South is their *natural* habitat, a place to which they totally belong. But because of her innate poise, dignity, and her realistic attitude toward life, she is able to rise above the benevolent paternalism that provided her with the luxury of believing that she belonged. She is a milestone on the road marking Faulkner's changing attitudes toward the Blacks in his novels: from the early indulgent, mild, and occasionally condescending treatment of them to a genuine expansion of his moral vision of them so that Blacks now appeared as distinct persons rather than as specters or phantasms (the "invisible man," in Ralph Ellison's felicitous phrase).

From an earlier and lazy reliance on the common assumption held by so many Southerners that Blacks were *easily knowable,* a false perception that came from a combination of fright and humaneness, Faulkner steadily advanced to recognition of injustices done to them, to recognition of the profound polarization of the races. The change is already evident in the contrast between Quentin's attitude toward Blacks and Jason's. Quentin can say of the Black jack-of-all trades, Deacon, "Now he can spend day after day marching in parades. If it hadn't been for my grandfather, he'd have to work like whitefolks" (p. 101). Not completely complimentary, but hardly as malicious as Jason, saying: "Like I say the only place for them is in the field, where they'd have to work from sunup to sundown. They can't stand prosperity or an easy job. Let one stay around white people for a while and he's not worth killing. They get so they can outguess you about work before your very eyes, like Roskus the only mistake he ever made was he got careless one day and died" (p. 312).

As Faulkner became more sensitive to the difficulties in approaching Blacks, he also developed (says Howe, *Major Writers of America*) "an admirable sense of reserve, a blend of shyness and respect." Besides his reverential treatment of Dilsey, he had only respect for Joe Christmas (the unfortunate mulatto in *Light in August*) and for Lucas Beauchamp (the Black hero of *Intruder in the Dust*). "No other American novelist watched them [the Blacks] so carefully and patiently; none other listened with such fidelity to the nuances of their speech; none other exposed his imagination so freely to discover their meaning for American life" (Howe).

COLES ON FAULKNER'S BLACKS. "No one interested in the individual as he encounters a society in swift transition will be bored by Mississippi or the Carolinas," says Robert Coles ("The South That Is Man's Destiny," from *Black and White in American Literature*). If some of its people hurt and exploit others, it is because the region itself has been ruthlessly exploited from one generation to the other. "Many of its people are poor, ignorant, and capable of an absurd kind of defensive chauvinism," Coles points out, "but many are sturdy, hardworking, kind people, so that as a whole every bit of Faulkner's vision seems sound."

BLACKS AND PRESERVATION OF THE ARISTOCRATIC IDEAL. With increasing sharpness of perception and growth of understanding, Faulkner also succeeded in mak-

ing us aware that Blacks as slaves often adopted the essence
of the aristocratic ideal (as they adopted Christianity, and
as they probably *adapted* many of their spirituals from
white Christian hymns) "with far more seriousness than
their masters, and that we, thanks to the tight telescoping
of American history, were but two generations from that
previous condition" (Ralph Ellison, *Black and White in
American Literature*).

FAULKNER AND BLACK MUSIC. Ellison also believes
that Faulkner explored more successfully than anyone else,
Black or white, certain aspects of Black humanity, partly
because of his extremely comprehensive exploration of the
South in general. Faulkner's impressions of Black music,
for example, are not epitomized by the flippant reference
Jason makes to the music of Beale Street, Memphis (p. 329),
but in the very fine examples of the quality, style, and range
of this music in *Sartoris*. Elnora, the Black house servant,
mops the floor to the accompaniment of snatches of spirituals.

Faulkner was perhaps more accurate than he realized
when he described the Blacks appropriating materials from
the general culture — spirituals, street songs sung by blind
singers, and singing-sermons — into their own style, a
process of hybridization of diverse materials which com-
petently defines the quality of American folksong, in particular the blues. In *The Sound and The Fury*, Faulkner is
perhaps more successful than any other writer (up to his
time) in describing the Black singing-sermon that Dilsey
is listening to on that Easter Sunday in 1928. The Reverend
Shegog begins in the standard speech of educated Southerners, then remembers the true nature of the congregation,
and suddenly changes to "Bredden en sistuhn!" The country dialect now takes over completely: " 'I got de ricklick-
shun en de blood of de lamb!' They did not mark just when
his intonation, his pronounciation became negroid [*sic*],

but they sat swaying a little in their seats as the voice took them into itself" (p. 368).

"It is a perceptive insight into the pluralistic pattern of American Negro life," Gene Bluestein observes, "and when the disguise is lifted Shegog fits immediately into the pattern of call and response which is basic to Negro folksong and folk sermons, the preacher half-speaking and half-singing, in concert with the occasional cries and melodic intonations of the congregation."

FAULKNER'S CREDO OF CO-EXISTENCE. "Let the white man give the Negro his rights, and the Negro teach the white man his endurance, and together we would dominate the United States," said Edmund Wilson (*Classics and Commercials*). There is no doubt that in later years Faulkner leaned more and more closely toward that credo for co-existence. His depth and fidelity in characterizing the Yoknapatawpha Blacks increased with the years; in *Soldier's Pay*, he was still willing to accept the myths of *his* own tribal past; in *The Sound and The Fury*, he began to question those myths; in *Go Down, Moses*, he was at last in open defiance of several of the stereotyped beliefs concerning the Blacks. During his last years, he was rejected by many of his fellow townsmen as too liberal, and accepted readily by Black intellectuals as not liberal enough. (See "A Word to Virginians," Feb. 20, 1958) "His essential liberalism on race can be questioned," says Sterling A. Brown (*A Century of Negro Portraiture in American Literature*). "There is no questioning, however, that in ploughing deeply into the soil of his single county, Faulkner was wise, prescient, and rewarding. What seems at first glance the familiar stereotyping becomes, on true reading, complex and revelatory, e.g. Dilsey is far more than the old mammy; Joe Christmas more than the tragic mulatto; Nancy Manigault more than the depraved 'wench.' . . . When he stands back and lets his Negro characters speak out and act out, Faulkner is right and often superb."

## ANNOTATED BIBLIOGRAPHY

### Anthologies, Speeches, and Interviews

Commins, Saxe, ed. *The Faulkner Reader*. New York: Random House, 1954. A generous sampling prepared by a man who had close contacts with Faulkner from 1936 to 1962, when Random House published the bulk of Faulkner's work.

Cowley, Malcolm, ed. *The Portable Faulkner*. New York: The Viking Press, 1946. Represented a veritable literary and critical breakthrough for Faulkner, a "revival" or "resurrection." Cowley's introduction invaluable, even more so in its "updating" of Faulkner's status as a writer based on his post-1945 books in Cowley's *revised 1967 edition*.

Grenier, Cynthia. "The Art of Fiction: An Interview with William Faulkner — September 1955." *Accent* XVI (Summer, 1956).

Gwynn, Frederick L. and Blotner, Joseph L., eds. *Faulkner in the University*. Charlottesville: The University of Virginia Press, 1959. Transcriptions of lectures, seminars, and interviews given by Faulkner during his years as writer-in-residence at the University of Virginia. The editors politely correct several of Faulkner's faulty recollections and misremembrances. In the main, authoritative.

Jeliffe, Robert A., ed. *Faulkner at Nagano*. Tokyo: The Kenkyusha Press, 1956. A transcript of the more important speeches and conferences of Faulkner's Japanese lecture tour. The literary values fortunately transcend whatever diplomatic values were intended for the tour by the State Department.

Stein, Jean. "William Faulkner: An Interview." *Writers at Work: The Paris Review Interviews*, 1st Series, ed. Malcolm Cowley (New York: The Viking Press, 1959; London: Martin Secker and Warburg, Ltd., 1959). Good, informative, free-wheeling talk by Faulkner in response to some incisive questioning.

## Faulkner Bibliographies

Meriwether, James B. "William Faulkner: A Check List," *The Princeton University Library Chronicle*, XVII (Spring, 1957). Valuable, so far as it goes; note in bibliography below how many new pieces of Faulkner criticism have come out *since 1957*.

Sleeth, Irene Lynn. "William Faulkner: A Bibliography of Criticism," *Twentieth-Century Literature*, VIII (April, 1962). Valuable for the few additional pieces of criticism available to this editor because of the time advantage; on the whole not preferable to Vickery.

Vickery, Olga W. "A Selective Bibliography," *William Faulkner: Three Decades of Criticism* (with Frederick Hoffman). East Lansing: The Michigan State University Press, 1960. More than a bibliography; a compendium of Faulkner criticism.

## Biographies, Memoirs, Reminiscences, and General Criticism

Baker, Carlos. *Ernest Hemingway: A Life Story*. New York: Chas. Scribner's Sons, 1969. Some early criticism — most of its generally fair — by one of Faulkner's most distinguished and immediate contemporaries.

Bluestein, Gene. "The Blues as a Literary Theme," *Black and White in American Literature*, reprinted from *Mas-*

*sachusetts Review,* III, 3, (Spring, 1962). Sources of Black music as illustrated in Faulkner's novels.

Brooks, Cleanth. *William Faulkner, The Yoknapatawpha Country.* New Haven: Yale University Press, 1963. Unusual insights and observations on Faulkner, his writings, and the South. Emphasis is on esthetic values.

Campbell, H. M. *William Faulkner, A Critical Appraisal.* New York: Cooper Square Publishers, Inc., 1971 (reprint of 1951 edition). Heavy on structural devices in the novels; especially valuable for *The Sound and The Fury.*

Coles, Robert. "The South That Is Man's Destiny," *Black and White in American Literature,* reprinted from *Massachusetts Review,* III, 3, (Spring, 1962). The exploited South as Faulkner saw it.

Coughlan, Robert. *The Private World of William Faulkner.* New York: Harper & Bros., 1954. For a reporter who never got to see Faulkner himself (but saw almost everybody else in Oxford), he succeeds in getting fairly deep into Faulkner's "private world." Originally appeared in *Life* magazine, hence highly readable in the popular style.

Cowley, Malcolm. *The Faulkner-Cowley File.* New York: Viking Press, 1966. An epistolary account (it contains 26 of Faulkner's letters to Cowley) of how Cowley got Faulkner to "cooperate" with him in editing *The Portable Faulkner.* The real Faulkner comes through.

Cullen, John B. and Watkins, Floyd C. *Old Times in the Faulkner Country.* Chapel Hill: The University of North Carolina Press, 1961. Could have been indispensable if the Brooks book (see above) had not come out.

Geismar, Maxwell. "A Rapt and Timid Power," a review of Irving Howe's *William Faulkner: A Critical Study* (New

York: Random House, 1962). *The Saturday Review*, July 12, 1952. Trenchant comments by the reviewer on Faulkner's Southern mystique and mythology. He liked the Howe book; so do we; it is very nearly the definitive *brief* study of Faulkner.

Faulkner, John. *My Brother Bill: An Affectionate Reminiscence*. New York: Trident Press, 1963. If John had been half the writer his brother Bill was, the book would have made for fascinating reading as well as for some authentic "I was there" information. Some of John's recollections are rather faulty.

Hamilton, Edith. A review of *Requiem for a Nun, The Saturday Review*, July 12, 1952. The book is a mere springboard from which the lady takes off to chastise Faulkner for his Puritanism and his extremely unfriendly attitude toward women (especially young ones).

Fiedler, Leslie A. "William Faulkner: Highbrow's Lowbrow," *No, in Thunder!* Boston: Beacon Press, 1960. Fiedler, more avant-garde than Geismar, takes off from where Geismar left off. Definitely not a "friendly" critic.

Frohock, W. M. "William Faulkner: The Private Versus the Public Vision," *The Novel of Violence in America*. Dallas: Southern Methodist University Press, 1950. How and why Faulkner gets away with such incredible violence in many of his novels.

Hoffman, Frederick J. *William Faulkner*. New York: Twayne Publishers, Inc., 1961. Solo effort (see next item) by a critic admirably qualified to analyze the idiosyncrasies of Faulkner's style and method.

Hoffman, Frederick J. and Vickery, Olga W., eds. *William Faulkner: Three Decades of Criticism*. East Lansing:

Michigan State University Press, 1960. One of the Faulknerite's best bets!

Hopper, Vincent F. "Faulkner's Paradise Lost," *Virginia Quarterly Review*, XXIII. Sees Faulkner preoccupied with the problem of evil, and compares his approach with that of Jonathan Swift and John Milton.

Howe, Irving. *William Faulkner: A Critical Study*. New York: Vintage Press, 1962. Not too subtle, not too abstruse, readable and reliable for professional and amateur Faulknerite.

Howe, Irving. *William Faulkner* (in *Major Writers of America*, Perry Miller, ed. New York: Harcourt Brace, Jovanovich, 1962). The student can use this brief but compendious critique of Faulkner's works and techniques until he is ready for the expanded and enlarged Howe.

Longley, John Lewis, Jr. *The Tragic Mask: A Study of Faulkner's Heroes*. Chapel Hill: The University of North Carolina Press, 1963. How to differentiate between tragic and pathetic hero, and why Faulkner's situations approach tragedy, but his heroes don't.

Millgate, Michael. *William Faulkner*. New York: Grove Press, 1961. No serious disagreement with other major Faulkner critics, but a highly individualistic approach to style and structure.

Miner, Ward L. *The World of William Faulkner*. Durham: Duke University Press, 1952. A guide to people, places, and events in real life that Faulkner transmuted into his Yoknapatawpha world.

Nilon, Charles H. *Faulkner and the Negro*. Boulder: University of Colorado Press, 1962. Fair, sincere analysis of Faulkner's treatment of Negro characters.

O'Connor, William Van. *The Tangled Fire of William Faulkner*. Minneapolis: University of Minnesota Press, 1954. Successfully extracts many poetic qualities in Faulkner's prose without scanting the basic tenets of the writer's private philosophy.

O'Connor, William Van. *William Faulkner*. Minneapolis: University of Minnesota Press, 1959. In this pamphlet on American Writers (a series), the reader will find a quick (but not sloppy) run-through of Faulkner's works.

O'Donnell, George Marion. "Faulkner's Mythology," *Kenyon Review*, I (Summer, 1939). Early recognition and identification of Faulkner's myth-making. Invaluable for understanding basic symbols and metaphors employed by Faulkner.

Price, Reynolds. "For Ernest Hemingway," *New American Review* 14 (1972). For more of a powerful contemporary's (and rival's) criticism of Faulkner.

Robb, Mary Cooper. *William Faulkner: An Estimate of His Contribution to the American Novel*. Pittsburgh: University of Pittsburgh Press, 1957. Many critics (and readers) may disagree with this "estimate."

Slatoff, Walter J. *Quest for Failure: A Study of William Faulkner*. Ithaca: Cornell University Press, 1960. Attempt to explain the *why* and *how* of Faulkner's frequent departures from standard language usage.

Swiggart, Peter. "Time in Faulkner's Novels," *Modern Fiction Studies*, V. Should be read along with Sartre's essay on time in *The Sound and The Fury*.

Tate, Allen. *Essays of Four Decades*. Chicago: Swallow Press, 1969. How Faulkner reversed the Aristotelian theory of tragedy.

Thompson, Lawrence. *William Faulkner: An Introduction and Interpretation.* New York: Barnes and Noble, Inc., 1963. At times, esoteric.

Vickery, Olga W. *The Novels of William Faulkner: A Critical Interpretation.* Baton Rouge: Louisiana State University Press, 1959. Insightful, in good taste, reliable.

Volpe, Edmund L. *A Reader's Guide to William Faulkner.* New York: The Noonday Press, 1964. Answer to a student's (and reader's) prayer. Volpe is one of the few critics who really understand Faulkner. Probably the nearest thing to a "concordance" to Faulkner.

Waggoner, Hyatt H. *William Faulkner: From Jefferson to the World*. Lexington: University of Kentucky Press, 1959. How Faulkner placed his own private world under the protection of his fictional world.

Warren, Robert Penn. *Faulkner, A Collection of Critical Essays.* Englewood Cliffs (N.J.): Prentice-Hall, 1967. Warren brings his fine judgments as a practicing author to his critical activities in selecting these very special essays.

Wilson, Edmund. *Classics and Commercials.* New York: Farrar, Straus & Giroux, Inc., 1950. Way back then, this giant among American critics recognized that there was something special about this offbeat novelist.

## On Faulkner's Technique

Aiken, Conrad. "William Faulkner: The Novel as Form," *The Atlantic Monthly,* November, 1939. According to Aiken, Faulkner was preeminently concerned with form, rather than content, and thus so much emphasis must be placed on the writer's technique.

Arthos, John. "Ritual and Humor in the Writing of William Faulkner," *Accent,* Autumn, 1948. The ritual stems from Faulkner's deep-seated religious convictions; the humor, from folklore and past and present Southern customs.

Beck, Warren. "William Faulkner's Style," *American Prefaces, Spring,* 1941. How Faulkner interrelated theme and structure.

Campbell, Harry M. "Structural Devices in the Works of Faulkner," *Perspective,* III. More on Faulkner's enigmatic style, with emphasis on the novel as form.

Riedel, F. C. "Faulkner as Stylist," *South Atlantic Quarterly,* LVI. Style comes first; narrative second.

Slatoff, Walter J. "The Edge of Order: The Pattern of Faulkner's Rhetoric," *Twentieth-Century Literature,* III (October, 1957). Convincing evidence that Faulkner's seemingly chaotic or overblown rhetoric was pre-planned, contrived, essential to the materials he used.

Zink, Karl E. "William Faulkner: Form as Experience," *South Atlantic Quarterly,* LIII. Slightly precious in approach, but of some value in understanding Faulkner's preoccupation with form.

## On The Sound and The Fury

Alpert, Hollis. "Old Times Are Not Forgotten," *The Saturday Review,* March 7, 1959. On *The Sound and The Fury* as a film. In spite of strong reservations about the typical Hollywood changes made in the basic Faulkner script, the review is favorable.

Backman, Melvin. *Faulkner: The Major Years.* Bloomington: Indiana University Press, 1966. See excellent analysis of the character of Quentin.

Bowling, Lawrence E. "Faulkner and the Theme of Innocence," *Kenyon Review*, XX (Summer, 1958). On the loss of innocence as a major theme of *The Sound and The Fury*.

Bowling, Lawrence E. "Faulkner: Technique of *The Sound and The Fury*," *Kenyon Review*, X (Autumn, 1948). Early but still valid introduction to the author's technique.

Brooks, Cleanth. "Man, Time, and Eternity," from *William Faulkner: The Yoknapatawpha Country*. New Haven: Yale University Press, 1963. Incisive study of both Quentins, with emphasis on courtly love.

Coindreau, Maurice. "Preface to *The Sound and The Fury*," *Mississippi Quarterly*, XIX (Summer, 1966). Coindreau sees the novel organized like a musical composition, the form approximating that of the symphony.

Collins, Carvel. "Christian and Freudian Structures," from "The Pairing of *The Sound and the Fury* and *As I Lay Dying*," *Princeton University Library Chronicle* XVIII (Spring, 1957). Southern Fundamentalists's approach to discovery of Christian parallels in the novel.

Collins, Carvel. "The Interior Monologues of *The Sound and The Fury*," *English Institute Essays*, 1952, ed. Allen S. Downer (New York: Columbia University Press, 1954). Emphasis on the novel's similarities to James Joyce, *Macbeth*, and Freud.

Cowan, Michael, ed. *Twentieth Century Interpretations of* THE SOUND AND THE FURY. Englewood Cliffs (N.J.): Prentice-Hall, 1968. Includes recent evaluations of the novel, plus generous sampling of some of the more celebrated "standards." Fine introduction.

Cross, Barbara. *"The Sound and The Fury:* The Pattern of Sacrifice," *Arizona Quarterly,* XVI. On Quentin as sacrificial victim *par excellence* and the concept of atonement.

Dauner, Louise. "Quentin and the Walking Shadow: The Dilemma of Nature and Culture," *The Arizona Quarterly,* XVIII (Summer, 1965). Invaluable guide to many of Faulkner's key symbols.

England, Martha W. "Quentin's Story: Chronology and Explication," *College English,* XXII (December, 1960). Logical reconstruction of the Quentin that was.

Howe, Irving. *William Faulkner: A Critical Study,* 2nd edition. New York: Random House, Inc., 1962. Howe discusses his reasons for preferring Benjy's section over Quentin's.

Hunt, John W. *William Faulkner: Art in Theological Tension.* Syracuse: Syracuse University Press, 1965. The sixty-page chapter on *The Sound and The Fury* is the longest single essay yet published on the novel. Covers fully Quentin's whole life; also, a detailed analysis of Jason.

Longley, John L. "The Legendary South: Toward a Theory of Epic Tragedy," in Cleanth Brooks, ed., *William Faulkner: The Yoknapatawpha Country* (New Haven: Yale University, 1963). On Benjy, Quentin, Jason, and Dilsey as possible candidates for tragic heroes. Dilsey most possible.

Lowrey, Perrin. "Concepts of Time in *The Sound and The Fury,*" from *English Institute Essays,* 1952, ed. Allen S. Downer (New York: Columbia University Press). Worthy complement to the classic Sartre essay (see below) on this subject. Main feature is the delineation of a "cyclical" progression that begins and ends the novel with Benjy.

Meriwether, James B. "Notes on the Textual History of *The Sound and The Fury*," *The Papers of the Bibliographical Society of America*, LVI (1962). Combines new insights into the novel's meaning with its history.

Millgate, Michael. *The Achievement of William Faulkner*. New York: Random House, 1966. Chapter on *The Sound and The Fury* discusses the novel's "twilight" qualities.

Powell, Sumner C. "William Faulkner Celebrates Easter, 1928," *Perspective*, II (Summer, 1949). Faulkner claimed the choice of Easter for *The Sound and The Fury* was unconscious; Powell nearly proves the choice had to be conscious.

Rabi. "Faulkner and the Exiled Generation," translated from the French of *Esprit* 175 (January, 1951). Good for what it says about the almost forgotten father, Jason Compson III.

Sartre, Jean-Paul. "On *The Sound and The Fury:* Time in the Work of Faulkner," *Literary and Philosophical Essays*, translated by Annette Michelson. London: Rider & Co., 1955. First published in 1939, this essay may be said to have "made" Faulkner. Although Sartre disagrees strongly with Faulkner's metaphysics, he has no quarrel with the author's technique.

Scott, Evelyn. *On William Faulkner's* THE SOUND AND THE FURY. New York: Jonathan Cape and Harrison Smith, Inc., 1929. Note the publication date of this book, one of the very earliest — and best — critiques on Faulkner's most important novel.

Slabey, Robert M. "The Romanticism of *The Sound and The Fury*," *The Mississippi Quarterly*, XVI (Summer, 1963). Good on Quentin as a romantic character.

Stewart, George R., and Backus, Joseph M. "Each in its Ordered Place: Structure and Narrative in Benjy's Section of *The Sound and The Fury*," *American Literature*, XXIX. Once the reader has mastered the Benjy section, the rest of the novel is relatively intelligible. This essay helps a lot.

Thompson, Lawrence. "Mirror Analogues in *The Sound and The Fury*," *English Institute Essays*, 1952. A valuable study of the relationship of some important symbols and the theme of the novel.

Vickery, Olga W. "Worlds in Counterpoint," Chapter 3 from *The Novels of William Faulkner: A Critical Introduction*. (Baton Rouge: Louisiana State University Press, 1964). How Quentin tried to bend experience into conformity with his system; also illustrates Jason's "calculating" (almost "legalistic" rather than "logical") approach to experience.

Wald, Jerry. "From Faulkner to Film," *The Saturday Review*, March 7, 1959. One has to admire this producer's *chutzpah* in choosing to convert *The Sound and The Fury* into film. But then, he performed the same good turn for D. H. Lawrence's *Sons and Lovers*.

Waggoner, Hyatt H. "Form, Solidity, Color," from *William Faulkner: From Jefferson to the World*. Lexington: University of Kentucky Press, 1959. An attempt to explore the more literary devices Faulkner may have consciously used to enhance his basic narrative. Generally follows critical lines laid down by Conrad Aiken.

Young, James Dean. "Quentin's Maundy Thursday," *Tulane Studies in English*, X (1960). In his search for Christian parallels, the author asks the reader to accept a Thursday

(June 2) in 1910 as part of the Easter Weekend (April 6, 7, 8) in 1928, to complete the four-part Christian celebration of the event.

## On Other Novels by Faulkner

*This section is arranged according to the chronological order in which the other novels appeared, instead of the critics' names, to provide a quick bibliography of Faulkner's novels.*

*Soldier's Pay* (1926). PRITCHETT, V. S. "Books in General," *New Statesman and Nation*, June 2, 1951. Since there is very little of a specific nature on this novel outside the larger critiques, Pritchett's is a rare treatment.

*Mosquitoes* (1927). VICKERY, OLGA W. A commentary on Faulkner's second novel, University of Kansas City *Review*, Spring, 1958. Clumsy, early Faulkner effort reevaluated in the light of Faulkner's enhanced reputation.

*Sartoris* (1929). SARTRE, JEAN-PAUL. *"Sartoris," Literary and Philosophical Essays*, London: Rider, 1955. Early, favorable recognition of novel that launched the Yoknapatawpha saga.

*As I Lay Dying* (1930). COLLINS, CARVEL. "Christian and Freudian Structures," from "The Pairing of *The Sound and The Fury* and *As I Lay Dying*," *Princeton University Library Chronicle* XVIII (Spring, 1957). Faulkner himself suggested the pairing of these two novels; herewith, some reasons for such a pairing. POWELL, HARRY M. "Experiment and Achievement: *As I Lay Dying* and *The Sound and The Fury*," *The Sewanee Review*, LI (Spring, 1943). More reasons.

*Sanctuary* (1931). COLE, DOUGLAS. "Faulkner's *Sanctuary*: Retreat from Responsibility," *Western Humanities Review*, XIV. Did Faulkner betray the public trust and his own better literary instincts in writing this sensational novel? Cole thinks so. FIEDLER, LESLIE. *Love and Death in the American Novel.* New York: Stein and Day, 1966. Fiedler has no quarrel with Faulkner's morality; he does have strong reservations about Faulkner's latent sadism and contempt for women, especially as manifested in *Sanctuary.*

*Light in August* (1932). CHASE, RICHARD. "The Stone and the Crucifixion: Faulkner's *Light in August,*" *Kenyon Review,* X (Autumn, 1948), 539-51. One of the definitive essays on the most "religious" of all of Faulkner's novels. NILSON, CHARLES H. *Faulkner and the Negro.* New York: The Citadel Press, 1965, 73-93. How Faulkner's treatment of Joe Christmas in this novel represented still one step further in the author's progress toward a more intelligent and sympathetic treatment of the Southern Blacks.

*Pylon* (1935). TORCHIANA, DONALD T. "Faulkner's *Pylon* and the Structure of Modernity," *Twentieth-Century Literature,* IV. Torchiana (and Hemingway) does not consider this novel a pot-boiler.

*Absalom, Absalom!* (1936). BROOKS, CLEANTH. "*Absalom, Absalom!*: The Definition of Innocence," *The Sewanee Review,* XIX. Next to *The Sound and The Fury,* Brooks considers this Faulkner's best novel. Clifton Fadiman found it almost impossible to get through the thicket of overlong sentences.

*The Unvanquished* (1938). KAZIN, ALFRED. "In the Shadow of the South's Last Stand," N.Y. Herald Tribune *Books,* February 20, 1938. A comprehensive, fairminded review of the book "hot of the press." For a change, an evaluation *not* attempted in retrospect.

*The Wild Palms* (1939). FADIMAN, CLIFTON. "Mississippi Frankenstein," *The New Yorker,* XIV, January 21, 1939.

Obviously a negative review. JACK, PETER M. "Mr. Faulkner's Clearest Novel," N.Y. Times *Book Review*, January 22, 1939. Obviously a favorable review.

*The Hamlet* (1940). WARREN, ROBERT PENN. "The Snopes World," *Kenyon Review*, III. A valuable analysis of the novel as well as a comprehensive explication of some of the devices Faulkner used in making the transition from the traditional Southerners (Sartoris, Compson, *et al*) to the Snopeses. A good introduction to the Snopes trilogy (*The Hamlet, The Town, The Mansion*).

*Go Down, Moses* (1942). LEWIS, R. W. B. "The Hero in the New World: William Faulkner's 'The Bear'," *Kenyon Review*, XIII. Since "The Bear" is the centerpiece of this novel, the reader should make every effort to understand it completely.

*Intruder in the Dust* (1948). LYTLE, ANDREW. "Regeneration for the Man," *The Sewanee Review*, LVII. Read this little essay before you see the film on TV. Any connection between this article (or the book) and the film is completely coincidental.

*Requiem for a Nun* (1951). HAMILTON, EDITH. "Requiem for a Nun," *The Saturday Review*, July 12, 1952. Hamilton's thesis: The values expressed in this novel are in sharp contradistinction to those expressed in Faulkner's Nobel Prize speech.

*A Fable* (1954). PRITCHETT, V. S. "Time Frozen," *Partisan Review*, XXI. Pritchett appreciates Faulkner's effort, but has polite reservations about the result. Even an Englishman finds it hard to be polite about a fiasco. STRAUMANN, HEINRICH. "An American Interpretation of Existence: Faulkner's *A Fable*," *Anglia*, LXXIII. One way to keep one's criticism polite is to plunge into metaphysics — like so.

*The Town* (1957). MERIWETHER, JAMES B. "The Snopes Revisited," *The Saturday Review,* April 27, 1957. See also Steven Marcus's "Snopes Revisited" (*Partisan Review,* XXIV) to see what all the enthusiasm for the Snopeses is all about. Is it because they are so much earthier and more realistic than the Compsons and the Sutpens, therefore much closer to us?

*The Mansion* (1959). BECK, WARREN. "Faulkner in *The Mansion*," *Virginia Quarterly Review,* XXXVI. With the third and final book in the trilogy out, the time was ripe for a summing-up of the Snopes saga. Beck shows how Faulkner neatly ties up most of the loose ends.

*The Reivers* (1962). BROOKS, CLEANTH. *William Faulkner, The Yoknapatawpha Country.* New Haven: Yale University Press, 1963. Brooks has a fine chapter on this, Faulkner's last novel. He likes the fact that Faulkner had regained his sense of humor and had returned to the "tall tale" that was so often the trademark of his better short stories.

———

# NOTES

**NOTES**

# NOTES

# MONARCH® NOTES *AND STUDY* GUIDES

## *ARE AVAILABLE AT RETAIL STORES EVERYWHERE*

In the event your local bookseller
cannot provide you with other
Monarch titles you want —

## ORDER ON THE FORM BELOW:

| TITLE # | AUTHOR & TITLE (exactly as shown on title listing) | PRICE |
|---------|---------------------------------------------------|-------|
|         |                                                   |       |
|         |                                                   |       |
|         |                                                   |       |
|         |                                                   |       |
|         |                                                   |       |
|         |                                                   |       |
|         |                                                   |       |
|         |                                                   |       |
|         |                                                   |       |
|         |                                                   |       |
|         |                                                   |       |
|         |                                                   |       |
|         |                                                   |       |
|         |                                                   |       |
|         | PLUS ADDITIONAL $1.00 PER BOOK FOR POSTAGE        |       |
|         | GRAND TOTAL                                       | $     |

**MONARCH® PRESS, a Simon & Schuster Division of Gulf & Western Corporation**
Mail Service Department, 1230 Avenue of the Americas, New York, N.Y.  10020

I enclose $ ........................... to cover retail price, local sales tax, plus mailing
and handling.

Name _____

(Please print)

Address _____

City _____ State _____ Zip _____

*Please send check or money order.  We cannot be responsible for cash.*

# Working
# for Yourself